HOW TO

PROPERTY INVESTING FOR BEGINNERS

BUY TO LET

A STEP BY STEP GUIDE ON HOW TO BUY A SAFE, SOLID, SOUND
& SECURE INVESTMENT PROPERTY

DAN COACHAFER

Creator: Dan Coachafer

Title: How To Buy To Let: Property Investing for Beginners: How to buy a safe, solid, sound and secure investment property.

Disclaimer

The advice provided in this publication is general advice only. It has been prepared without taking into account your objectives, financial situation or business needs. Before acting on this advice you should consider the appropriateness of the advice, having regard to your own objectives, financial situation and business needs. To the maximum extent permitted by law, the author and publisher disclaim all responsibility, and liability to any person, arising directly or indirectly from any person taking or not taking action, based on the information in this publication.

'new2property' or its agents do not provide legal, investment, mortgage, loan, tax, financial or accountancy advice, and any general information provided by new2property or its agents should be qualified with a professional. The professional services new2property recommends are independent organisations and any advice provided by the recommended professional services is done by their own entities.

To my grandparents Albert and Phillis Lackenby. By leaving me my first investment property, they gave me the belief that anything is possible and allowed me to chase my dreams.

To my dad Allan Coachafer. Without your unwavering support, sacrifice, and belief in me, this work would not have been possible.

Contents

IMPORTANT!
READ THIS FIRST!

Dear Investor,

May name is Dan Coachafer and I`m going to be your buy to let, (BTL) mentor.

I`d like to start by giving you an idea of what to expect and how to best work with this book to help you get the most out of it.

Unlike others, this book is written in a way to guide both new and experienced property investors to purchase a safe, solid, sound and secure 'buy to let' investment property.

I`m going to be sharing my knowledge and experience gained over 13 years of investing in property and passing on what I have learnt whilst building my portfolio of 15 buy to lets, including 1 mini HMO.

At my company: 'new2property', I am the 'buy to let' mentor where I guide clients through every step of the buy to let process. This book is written to guide you too.

The end goal is for you to have purchased a property. You will gain the knowledge and skills required to grow a profit-making portfolio and have learnt everything you need to know to become a successful 'buy to let' property investor.

To get the best out of this book you will need to take your time; this isn't going to be an overnight read and there is a lot of information to digest and absorb.

Thank you for purchasing my book and for giving me the chance to help you on your journey.

Sincerely

Dan

P.S. You`ll benefit most if you read this book straight through, from cover to cover, completing each task as they arise, instead of hopping around.

Ready? Let's get cracking!

ONE

Who is your mentor?

I n my mid 20`s, back in 2007, whilst in Australia "discovering myself", I was lucky enough to inherit my first property: a 3 bed, mid- terrace in Newark, Nottinghamshire, housing Lou, a sitting tenant paying £16 cash a week in rent, (don't ask!) After swatting up on the council's fair rent policies, the rent was increased to the average amount for the area and I was introduced to a passive income.

I continued to work and live overseas whilst collecting a hassle-free passive income of £400 per calendar month and realised this was an easy way to earn money. Enthused and excited by my new venture, I worked hard and saved up enough for my next deposit. I quickly discovered that, without a "real" job, I would struggle to get a mortgage.

Thankfully my supportive parents stepped in and helped by taking out a loan for home improvements. I used the loan money plus my own deposit and bought my second property. Passive income was now £800 pcm; however, all profits were used to pay my parents back.

With no further loan options, I was stumped and had no choice but to save and wait until I had a full-time job, or so I thought.

On a sunny afternoon, whilst playing water polo in a backpacker's hostel in Australia, I met Vinny: still a close friend today. Vinny spoke of a mortgage adviser who could secure mortgages for the most un-mortgageable. On my next trip back to the UK I contacted Cheryl Marshall, an independent, all market mortgage adviser based in Essex, and, lo and behold, she pulled it off; I had just secured my third property.

Previously my idea of a great 'buy to let' property was exactly the same spec. as my first: in the same town and even on the same street. I knew nothing about return on investment and my strategy was to buy 10 properties, pay them all off, sell them and become a millionaire: every young man's dream right?

Realising there could be something in property investing I decided to take a season off to educate myself and secured a job in a UK estate agent. Within the branch was the sales team, which I joined, a lettings department and a mortgage adviser. I also hit the books hard and expanded my network and knowledge by rubbing shoulders with like-minded property investors. I attended networking events and invested in property education. Six months passed, I acquired property number 4 and then returned to work overseas.

Whilst abroad I worked as a corporate sales coach where I mentored team managers. During my professional career I have undergone extensive training and have over 10 years' experience in up-skilling professionals, developing confidence and systemising processes.

Over the next few years, I continued to read, watch videos and listen to podcasts. I also fully researched my patch; I analysed every property that came to market in the area I was investing, and I flew back approximately every six months to view and make offers on properties of interest.

Over a 10 + year period learning about investing in property, trying and testing a variety of ideas and methods and taking practical steps to build a profit generating portfolio, at 39 I purchased my 11th property. This was 3 months before my 10 year goal of owning 10 properties before my 40th birthday. I am still 40 and completed on property number 15 last month (April 2020).

I now have a SMART (Specific, Measurable, Achievable, Realistic, and Timed) goal and I'm no longer hitting and hoping.

I believe that education is key. Knowing your SMART goal, strategy, capabilities and having the confidence to take action will allow you to achieve your personal target.

If I knew what I know now when I bought my first property, I would have been retired long ago.

Today I'm helping new or experienced investors through each and every step of the buying process. I work alongside a team of professionals who assist in supporting and guiding clients to buy a sound, safe, secure and solid investment property.

If you stick with me through this book, I'll help you too.

TWO

What do you want to achieve?

In my opinion, setting a SMART goal is the very first thing anyone looking to invest in property needs to get nailed.

What exactly do you want to achieve from investing in property?

SMART stands for Specific, Measurable, Achievable, Realistic and Timed.

It is important to be very clear with your goal. Many new and even experienced investors waste time, effort, energy and money going around in circles as they don`t have a clear and defined property investing goal.

Let me ask you this: have you ever hit the road without a named destination in mind, if not why not? And if so, did you end up in the best, most perfect location for you at that time?

9/10 'new to property' investors don't have an exact destination in mind and therefore they fail. If you don't know where you are going how will you ever know if you have arrived?

"So, how do I plan a SMART goal", I hear you ask?

Easy, write it down, as loosely as you like, in fact simply answer this question: What do you want to achieve from investing in property? Don't overthink it, don't try and make it complicated, just write it down.

At this stage your goal doesn't need to be perfect; having anything down on paper is better than nothing.

However, by making your goal SMART, you will give yourself the best possible chance of success.

Let's work together to make your goal SMART.

S – Specific: let's use an example that you may have written down.

I want to give up my job and use the money I make from property income as a wage.

When you re-write your goal, drill it down to create something like this:
I would like to achieve a passive net income of £2000 per month generated from rental properties. This income will replace my current wage and I will no longer rely on my career to fund my lifestyle.

Great start, next up is **M – Measurable:** how will you know when you have achieved your goal?

You could write something like this:

For me to hit my goal I will consistently (more than three consecutive months) receive £2,000 passive net income on a monthly basis, this income will be generated solely from rental properties. I will have quit my current job and be relying solely on income generated from a property portfolio to fund my lifestyle.

Then **A – Achievable:** is your goal achievable?

You could write:

From my research, a BTL property costing £100,000 in my area will generate a minimum of £250 net income pcm. I will need to acquire 8 BTL properties to generate a minimum of £2,000 net income pcm. I will need approximately £240,000 for deposits and costs.

I can release £200,000 of equity from my residential property and over the next 2 years, I can save £40,000. But is this Realistic?

R – Realistic: It's important to do your research and ensure that your goal is realistic. I suggest asking questions such as: has my goal been achieved before? Is my research and data accurate? Do I have the funds? Do I have the time? Am I skilled in what is needed?

You may write:

I know more than 5 people who have achieved this exact goal in my chosen area. I have allowed enough time to acquire the properties needed. I have the funds to acquire 6 properties and can save enough from my corporate wage for the final two properties, as a backup plan I will try to acquire properties below market value and re-finance to release further funds. However, I do still need to find the properties and to understand the best properties to buy, where to buy and how it all works. To ensure I up-skill in these areas I will work with a buy to let property mentor who has already achieved my goal.

And finally, how long will it take you to achieve your goal?
T – Timed:

You could state,
It takes approximately 6 months to acquire 1 property, I need to acquire 8 properties and have given myself 4 years, this is 2 per year and 1 every six months. I will achieve my set goal within the next 4 years. My last day at work will be on 12.12.20.

And there you have it; now you have a SMART goal. In this example, the investor is looking for BTL, single let properties costing approximately £100,000 which will generate a net (minimum) income of £250 pcm. To achieve this goal two properties a year are needed over a four-year period totalling 8 properties. The investor has the time and funds, they will become educated about which properties will work best by working with a mentor; and the investor's goal has been achieved by others. When a passive net income of £2,000 pcm. is achieved consistently over a 3-month period the investor will have achieved their goal.

Remember your goal needs to be personal and tailored to you.

Task: Spend some time writing down your property investing goal. If it`ll help, head over to the 'new2property' SMART goal template at this address:
https://www.new2property.co.uk/smart-goal-template
Then rewrite your initial goal making it SMART.

THREE

Strategy setting

Now you have outlined your SMART goal you need a strategy to help you achieve it.

Having a defined step by step strategy is the key to ensuring you achieve your property investing goal.

Many new and inexperienced investors waste time, effort, energy and money working on tasks that are not moving them closer to their goal.

Once you have a route planned out, getting to your chosen destination becomes much easier.

By devising a step by step strategy, you will eliminate the possibility of veering down the wrong path.

A strategy helps to keep you on track and remain focused on tasks that will get you closer to your property goal.

Did you know, if put on the spot most property investors would not be able to clearly present their investment strategy?

Having a clear step by step strategy will put you closer to achieving success than most.

Check out the example below and start thinking about the steps that you will need to take to achieve your own goal.

1. Define a SMART goal and outline a step by step strategy.
2. Speak to a mortgage adviser about refinancing residential property to release funds.
3. Speak to a specialist property accountant and decide whether it is better to buy as a limited (LTD) company or by using your own name as a sole trader.
4. Set up a LTD company, or register as a sole trader.
5. Open a business bank account.
6. Refinance residential property.
7. Obtain a decision in principle ready to offer on properties.
8. Decide on a tenant pool and a property type/specification.
9. Decide on an investment area.
10. Perfect and systemise search area and filters on Rightmove.
11. Contact all local estate agents and deal sources.
12. View properties.
13. Offer and negotiate on the chosen property.
14. Instruct a solicitor.
15. Select a RICS surveyor and have a survey completed.
16. Select a suitable letting agent.
17. Set and forget property number 1.
18. Start again at step number 12 repeatedly until secured 7 additional properties.
19. Monitor funds being generated, allow 6 months to pass to reach the point at which £2,000 pcm from property is being generated.
20. Quit the day job.

Task: Spend some time writing down what steps you th nk you need to take to hit your property investing goal. If it`ll help head over to the 'new2property' strategy template at this address:
https://www.new2property.co.uk/strategy-template

Top Tip: At this stage, your strategy won`t be perfect but as your knowledge develops you will be able to add to your strategy ensuring you remain on the path to success.

FOUR

Setting up for success

Being set up for success from day one is paramount when you start out investing in property. If you get this step wrong it will cost you time, effort, energy and money further down the line.

In this chapter, we will explore both buying as a limited company and in your own name and we will delve into the pros and cons of each.

At this stage, I do need to point out that the information in this chapter can only be used as guidance rather than advice, I am not FCA accredited and the final task in this chapter is for you to contact a property specialist accountant to ensure you receive professional advice before moving on.

Before we investigate buying in your own name or in a limited company it's important to be clear on the facts.

Here is what we know...

The current (April 2020) personal tax-free allowance is £12,500 meaning you can earn £12,500 in your own name and not pay any tax.

If you earn over £12,500 and below £50,000 you are classed as a lower rate taxpayer and you will pay 20% tax on all earnings over £12,500.

If you earn over £50,000 and below £150,000 you are classed as a higher rate taxpayer and will pay 40% tax on all earnings over £50,000.

If you earn over £150,000 you are classed as an additional-rate taxpayer and will pay 45% tax on all earnings over £150,000.

Corporation tax (the tax you pay on your earnings as a limited company) is currently (April 2020) 19% and is maintained at this "flat-rate" irrespective of the level of income received into the company.

You can "vote" (pay) dividends to yourself (the return of profit from the company after corporation tax and expenses/liabilities are taken into account) from a limited company, of which the first £2,000 is taxed at 0% annually; however this does count towards your annual income but does not use up your basic rate tax band allowance.

If you pay yourself a wage from a limited company you will pay both corporation tax of 19% and income tax at 20%, 40% or 45% depending on your personal earnings.

Please note that these guidelines are correct at the time of publication (April 2020) and are subject to review/change by the government.

Should you always buy in a limited company?

Using a limited company is of restricted benefit to a basic rate (20%) taxpayer. Although it should be noted that if an investor's long-term intentions are to grow a substantial portfolio, a limited company is a good vehicle, even if the advantages of using a limited company are somewhat limited initially.

A more obvious benefit arises once an individual exceeds the higher rate tax threshold, which can be achieved with a mix of property income and personal income. It is also at this higher-rate level of income that the *section 24 rules come into p ay.

Section 24 restrictions do **not** apply to limited companies so in this sense they offer a further advantage. Finally, you should not forget the limitation of liability itself that the company status brings with it.

*Section 24 was introduced in April 2017 and is being phased in over a 4-year period. It means that landlords will no longer be able to claim mortgage interest, or any other property finance, as tax-deductible. Instead, rental profit will be taxed with a maximum deduction for finance costs of 20%, the basic tax rate, by 2021. The full name of the act is Section 24 of the Finance (No. 2) Act 2015.

When is it best to buy in a limited company?

A limited company is a great investment vehicle but only if it's right for you.

A limited company vehicle can result in considerable tax savings for a higher rate (40%) taxpayer, and this is especially so if the investor is prepared to retain some of their profits in the limited company. It is worth noting that the maximum tax-saving can be achieved by leaving all profits within the company, although this clearly depends on the investor's investment and tax strategy.

Investors following this strategy often use these accumulated or retained profits within the company to fund future investments.

If an investor only plans on buying one 'buy to let' property a limited company is not likely to be the best option, however, if an investor does choose the limited company route, it's important to remember monthly income will be reduced due to the accountancy, admin and compliance fees associated with owning a limited company.

Also statistically speaking – a one-time investor is more likely to sell a property after a few years and on doing so will get hit with the 'double tax effect' if the property is sold from a limited company. i.e. capital gains on the sale and then followed by higher-rate dividend tax when subsequently extracting the sale-proceeds from the company.

The chances are, that if an investor plans to grow a portfolio of any decent size (5+ buy to let investment properties) then a limited company is likely to be the best way to go.

A 'buy to let' might not be the best option
A buy to let investment property doesn't always make financial sense.

It is possible, depending on an investor's goal and circumstance, that a 'buy to let' property is not always financially the best option.

Overall an investor must consider tax and investment strategy, investor's tax rate, section 24, who else is investing, etc. Specific circumstances are ultimately what will dictate if a property investment is a good financial move.

In summary
Setting up correctly now will ensure success in the future.

20% taxpayer – many lower rate taxpayers tend to buy in their personal name, although a limited company may be considered if the investor is looking to grow a larger portfolio over the long-term.

40% taxpayer – many higher rate taxpayers and serious investors tend to buy in a limited company. They expect decent tax savings if some (or especially all) profits are left in the company and they plan to buy more than one property. This route is also especially good due to the section 24 advantage on the mortgage-interest.

That being said, for a one-off investment, many investors would buy in their own name – even if they are higher-rate taxpayers, mainly due to the level of admin, the increased accountancy fees, and to mitigate the double-tax if subsequently selling.

Now it's over to you...

Task: Before you continue your property investing journey it's important that you speak to a property specialist accountant who will be able to advise you on whether to buy in a limited company or in your own name.

For a free consultation with the 'new2property' specialist accountant visit the team page of the new2propety website *https://www.new2property.co.uk/team* where you wil find full contact details and a link to our specialist property accountants` independent website

.

FIVE

The limited company route

I f, after speaking to a specialist property accountant, the limited company route is best for you then you have two options.

Option 1 - You can instruct an accountant to set up the company for you, an accountant will typically charge between £100 - £150 for this service.

Option 2 - You can set up the company yourself. The total cost of setting up a new limited company online is £12 which can be paid by debit or credit card or with a PayPal account.

It typically takes 24 hours for the company to be incorporated (registered).

If you do choose to set up a new company yourself the steps below are for guidance only and are not to be taken as financial advice. It is advisable to have a professional set up a new LTD company to ensure accuracy of information and structure.

You'll need at least 3 pieces of personal information about yourself and your shareholders or guarantors which can include:
- Town of birth.
- Mother's maiden name.
- Father's first name.
- Telephone number.
- National insurance number.
- Passport number.

Firstly, you will need a company name, your company name cannot be the same as:
- Another registered company's name.
- An existing trademark.

Your name must usually end in either 'Limited' or 'Ltd'.

Head over to the government companies house website **https://beta.companieshouse.gov.uk/company-name-availability** and enter your new company name, you will see if your company name already exists.

If your chosen name doesn't exist, click register a private limited company online.

You will be asked if you want to register a new company, if the company is new and then you will be taken through the steps to set up your company.

You'll be issued a Government Gateway ID. Keep this safe as you'll need it to pass to your accountant and to log in to your online business account.

During the set up you will be asked to register an official address, your home address can be your office address if you don't have an office.

You will also be asked for a 'SIC code' is a Standard Industrial Classification code. These are used by Companies House to classify the type of economic activity in which a company or other type of business is engaged.

For simply buying and letting property, the SIC code is – 68209: "Other letting and operating of own or leased real estate".

Please note you will need a separate SIC code for each service your company provides. SIC codes can be added during the set-up process.

If you are unsure on any part of the LTD Company set up, I strongly advise that you seek guidance from a property specialist accountant who can ensure you are set up correctly.

SIX

All About Finance

Should you buy with cash?

One of the biggest advantages of buying an investment property in cash is not having to pay back a loan or interest on borrowed money. However, does this outweigh the positives of using leverage (a mortgage)?

Let's take a look at some further advantages:
- It's a common belief that a seller is more likely to accept a lower offer if the offer is in cash. However, it`s worth keeping in mind that not all sellers need to move quickly, and some are more than happy to wait it out for a better deal.
- As a cash buyer, the mortgage application process and costs associated with using a mortgage would be avoided. This would make purchasing a property far easier, cheaper and quicker.

What about the disadvantages?
- As a cash investor, a lower return on investment will be achieved as increased capital will have been paid into the deal.

- If an investor puts all their capital into only one deal, they will be solely reliant on one revenue stream.

What is leverage?

Leveraging is using other people's money (typically the banks in the form of a mortgage) to acquire assets, which in turn make a higher return on the initial investment.

If using leverage to invest in a 'buy to let' property, profit will be made on an asset that has been paid for predominantly with someone else's (the banks) money.

One of the advantages of buying an investment property using a mortgage is the increased return on the capital that has been invested.

If the 'buy to let' property is purchased within a limited company an investor can offset the mortgage interest against the rental income and this provides a huge tax advantage.

Let's look at a couple of examples.

A cash purchase

An investor buys an investment property for £100,000 which achieves a 7% gross annual yield.
£7,000 per year is earned before costs.
Costs (management fee, maintenance, insurance, repairs etc.) come to £1,500.
The net income is £5,500 or 5.5% return on investment (before income tax).

A purchase using a mortgage

If the same deal was recreated using a 75% loan to value with an interest-only mortgage.

Meaning £25,000 of the £100,000 was used as a deposit.

The investor would still receive £7,000 gross annual income.

Costs would still be £1,500.

If the mortgage interest was 3.75%.

Totalling an annual payment of £2,812.5 in mortgage interest.

The net income is now £2,687 or 10.75% return on investment (before income tax).

If this was replicated across 4 'buy to let' properties using the £100,000 as deposits, the annual net profit would be almost £10,750, double what it would be if only one property was purchased in cash.

Also, if one of the properties experienced a void in tenancy, there would still be rental income coming in from the other properties.

The downside to this scenario is that there are mortgage payments that must be met, whether the properties are let or not and there will now also be 4 mortgages to repay and a small portfolio of properties to manage.

Repayment mortgages

A repayment mortgage is the typical mortgage product used when buying a residential property. With a repayment mortgage part of the loan as well as the interest is repaid on a monthly basis. At the end of the term, the entire loan and interest is paid off.

The advantage of a repayment mortgage is that, at the end of the term, there is nothing further to pay.

The disadvantage of a repayment mortgage is that monthly repayments will be higher than on an interest-only mortgage, and the extra capital could be used for additional investments.

Interest only mortgages

With an interest-only mortgage, only the interest is paid on a monthly basis for the term of the loan. The amount borrowed isn't due until the end of the term. Interest-only mortgages are typically used by property investors.

The advantage of an interest-only mortgage is that monthly payments are less than they would be on a repayment mortgage.
Investors typically use the capital saved by not paying off the loan, to reinvest in additional assets.

The disadvantage of an interest-only mortgage is that the loan amount will still have to be re-paid at the end of the term.

Not all mortgage lenders offer interest-only products and those that do have stricter criteria for the lending. Lenders usually ask for a higher minimum deposit, typically 25% for 'buy to let' mortgages. A lender will also be interested in how the borrower plans to repay the loan amount at the end of the term.

How do you pay back an interest only mortgage?

There are several options for repaying an interest-only mortgage, however the strategy chosen will depend heavily on an investor's goal and personal circumstance.

Below are a few ideas to help you build on your own personal plan.

- Re-mortgage to a better mortgage rate, switch to a repayment mortgage and repay the loan over a longer term to make monthly payments more affordable.
- Sell the property to raise the funds and pay back the loan in a lump sum at the end of the term.

- Pay into an investment plan which can then be used to pay off the loan amount in a lump sum at the end of the term.

It's also possible to make lump sum overpayments on some mortgage products.

At the time of publication it is possible to leave buy to let properties to executors in a will. Everything can be left to a spouse free of inheritance tax and there is a £325,000 tax-free allowance per person, plus up to £125,000 extra if an estate includes a family home and the property is left to the children. If a widow or widower inherited their late spouse's entire estate, it's possible to claim the late spouse's tax-free allowance, meaning up to £900,000 can be left tax-free.

Do you qualify for a 'buy to let' mortgage?
Speaking generally: if the criteria below are ticked then an investor shouldn't have a problem qualifying for a 'buy to let' mortgage.

- UK passport.
- UK bank account.
- Permanent UK residency.
- Permanent employment earning a minimum annual income of £25,000 with a UK registered employer or
- Self-employed with a minimum of 3 years of accounting history.

When mortgage lenders make the decision to lend or not typically the below points are considered.

- Personal income.
- Credit rating/history.
- Amount of investment properties already owned.
- Ownership of residential property.
- Deposit available.
- Monthly rental income on investment property.

- Property type.

> **Task:** Head over to the Experian website:
> **https://www.experian.co.uk/** where you can run a free
> online credit check and check your own credit rating.

What is an AIP / DIP?

A mortgage in principle is also known as a Decision in Principle (DIP), Agreement in Principle (AIP) or a mortgage promise. This is a statement from a lender saying that they'll lend a certain amount.

A mortgage in principle can be used to prove affordability to a seller, which could help if the seller is deciding between more than one buyer.

It's important to note that an AIP is offered in principle only. When making a formal application for the mortgage itself, the lender has the right to change the details of the deal, or they may decide not to grant the loan (for example, if financial circumstances have changed). If a long period of time is left between obtaining a mortgage in principle and applying for a mortgage the interest rates may have changed, or a better deal could be found elsewhere.

It is advisable to have an agreement in principle before starting to offer; being able to produce an AIP will increase the chances of an offer being accepted. It's common for estate agents to continue to actively advertise a property until an AIP is produced.

A mortgage broker would normally apply for an AIP on their client's behalf (the buyer), they will require:
- 2 forms of identification.
- The approximate purchase price of a property.
- The estimated rental income the property will generate.

- Past 3 months bank statements and payslips as proof of income.

The application is typically submitted online, which triggers a credit search and basic information check. Some lender portals give an instant result, others can take a couple of hours. The application can be denied, approved or it may be highlighted to be manually checked, if a manual check is required this can take approximately 48 hours.

Complex cases and some smaller building societies require a paper form to be submitted which will take longer to be assessed.

Once an agreement in principle is approved the broker typically forwards a copy to their client who in turn sends it on to the estate agent or seller to prove their lendability.

An AIP is typically valid for 30-90 days depending on the lender.

When choosing a mortgage, it's important to get the best product to suit your needs. A skilled and experienced mortgage adviser should be able to present the most suitable solutions. Typically, investors consider the factors below before making their decision.

- Early repayment fees.
- Length of the loan.
- Length of the fixed term.
- Fixed or variable rates.
- Any fees, and if they are included or not.
- Total cost, over the product term, factoring in any fees, set up costs and monthly payments.

Interview with a mortgage advisor

I interviewed Cheryl Marshall the Director of Chelmer Mortgages who I have worked with for 12+ years. Cheryl was able to source me my very first mortgage when I was told by many it wasn't possible. She has a wealth of knowledge when it comes to anything mortgage related. I asked Cheryl:

How long have you been in the mortgage industry and what got you into it in the first place?

I have been a mortgage advisor for nearly 15 years. I started working in an estate agency when I was in my early twenties, I became very interested in the industry and decided the mortgage route could be an interesting career. I completed the training passed the exams and the rest is history.

What is an independent mortgage advisor?

An advisor who has access to the whole market, basically they can work with all the banks and building societies offering loans and can choose a provider to work with. Some mortgage advisors only have access to a select panel of mortgage companies. If you go direct to your bank you'll only be offered their own products. An independent mortgage advisor can shop around for the best product to suit their client; they can pursue the best rate and they are more likely to be impartial with their advice.

Should you work with a mortgage advisor who had experience with buy to let investors?

Mortgage advisers tend to work with two types of clients: residential buyers and investors. There are often restrictions with buy to let mortgages. Investors have a completely different goal and mind set to clients buying a residential property. Understanding the investment niche, how investors work, what they are working to achieve etc. really helps pair them up with the best product. A mortgage advisor who has only dealt with residential clients would not be best suited to take on investors; it's a completely different ball game and one that takes time to fully understand.

Are specialist investment mortgage advisors more expensive?

Some advisors charge a fee for giving advice or an arrangement *fee. If the scenario is complex and additional work is involved then the fee may be higher, personally I don`t charge an extra fee.*

What other costs should I expect and when will they come?

The largest costs of purchasing a property will usually be the deposit and maybe the renovations. But if we look at the purchase costs only, then the deposit will be up there as a major cost. Typically, you`ll need a 25% deposit for a buy to let purchase. There may be a lender's arrangement fee, this is to set up the product, some lenders don`t charge but those that do can charge anything up to 3% of the loan amount. It`s important to factor this cost in and workout the overall mortgage cost. There may be a valuation fee. You will also have the cost of a survey, legal fees, stamp duty and some agents are even charging buyers to purchase a property now.

What happens when I have selected a mortgage advisor and product?

The mortgage company will want to check the property is secure to lend on and that it's in a good state of repair. They will, as part of your application, instruct a surveyor to value the property.

The surveyor will have a general look around to make sure the property is in a good state of repair and that the agreed purchase price matches the current market value. A report will be generated for the lender and the property will be checked to ensure it's suitable and secure to lend on.

Many customers also have a more in-depth survey carried out to check damp, movement etc. to mitigate risk later down the line.

If the valuation report matches the agreed purchase price is the mortgage guaranteed?

Once the lender is happy with the valuation report and you as a client, they will fully agree the mortgage. At this point you`ll *receive a full mortgage offer and legal proceedings can commence.*

Does an investor need to meet face to face with a mortgage advisor?

Not necessarily, some clients do like to meet face to face however it's not a necessity. Documents can be sent electronically, and communication can be via phone and email.

Here are some questions I suggest you ask a mortgage advisor before instructing them:

- *Do you have access to all lenders and if not, who don`t you work with?*
- *What percentage of your clients are investors?*
- *Do you charge a fee for giving advice or an arrangement fee?*

Top Tip: Finding a knowledgeable, skilled and trustworthy mortgage advisor can be challenging however its worth doing your research, asking for recommendations and shopping around.

You can watch the full interview by searching "UK buy to let mortgages explained" on the new2property You Tube channel and to find out more about Cheryl and to contact her visit the "team" page of the new2propery website.
https://www.new2property.co.uk/team

Task: Before you continue your property journey speak to a mortgage advisor. I suggest you find an all market, independent mortgage advisor who will be able to advise you on non-bias mortgage options.

The Power of Inflation

Inflation is an increase in the general price level of goods and services over time. Although often misunderstood and frequently overlooked, inflation can be a 'buy to let' property investor's best friend. Understanding how inflation works should be high on every property investor's priority list.

If used well, inflation can make a property investor very wealthy but equally if ignored can leave anyone poor. Inflation punishes savers and rewards those who utilise its power.

The most well-known indicator of inflation is the Consumer Price Index (CPI), which measures the percentage change in the price of a basket of goods and services consumed by households.

In the early 1970s the average price of a loaf of bread was 8 pence; in the shops today a loaf is an average of £1.20 pence. Bread hasn't become more expensive to produce it's actually now cheaper, the difference in price is due to inflation.

Since the year 2000, inflation has increased at an average of 2.8% annually, meaning: something that cost £100 last year will cost £102.80 this year. This doesn't sound like anything to get excited about however over the long term the increase can make a significant difference, especially when investing in property.

There are several reasons why we see an increase in inflation, the most common reasons are:
- Supply and demand — If there is more demand than supply the price of the goods or service in demand goes up as the general public will be prepared to pay more.
- Quantitative easing (QE) — This is an increase in the country's money supply, basically when the government adds more money to the economy.

- The UK government target inflation is 2% per year and the economy benefits greatly from a gradual increase.

The government encourages inflation as it helps the economy grow. Inflation also helps to erode the government debt which, as we all know, isn't small.

It's a common belief that inflation doesn't really matter if wages rise at the same rate or higher than inflation, however, inflation has a huge effect on savings. If a savings account is providing no interest, then the savings in the account are decreasing in value as time passes. When the savings are extracted at a later date, they will be worth less than when it was initially banked.

Most saving accounts offer an interest rate that is lower than inflation, meaning that savings in the bank are slowly becoming worth less over time. Unless the interest rate on the savings is higher than 2.8% (average annual inflation rate increase) then a saver is becoming poorer over time by saving money.

Inflation is seen as an invisible savings thief; the money being taken isn't seen but the value is invisibly decreasing over time.

Investments need to be generating more than inflation for a portfolio to simply stay afloat.

It's worth remembering, as an investor, when working out return on investment, inflation should be subtracted to get an accurate view.

Let's look at an example
With a 10% return on investment.
Once the rate of inflation has been subtracted 10% - 2.8%.
The actual return being generated is 7.2%.

This example makes inflation sound bad, however as a property investor inflation can be used as a very powerful tool.

It's important for property investors to acknowledge that inflation will always occur so understanding and leveraging it is the winning formula to success.

Rents tend to rise in line with inflation.

If income increases with inflation, then renters have more disposable income, meaning they will be willing to pay more rent. An investment property can be an inflation-beating asset.

By combining inflation with leverage, property investors can do very well, financially.

Debt is eroded by inflation
Inflation becomes even more exciting when an investor uses leverage. Not only is the debt on the property decreasing overtime the property is also increasing in value, both with the investor doing nothing.

Example: £75,000 was borrowed and an interest-only mortgage product was used putting down a 25% deposit (£25,000). None of the debt was paid off over a 25-year period the total amount owed at the end of the term would be the same amount but worth far less.

On average, house prices across the UK rise faster than inflation, meaning that even if an investor put all their hard-earned saving into one buy to let property, they would be in a far better position than if the money was saved in a bank account.

With the value of debt going down and the price of property going up, property investing can create exceptional long-term wealth.

Task: Head over to Rightmove's website: sold prices section: *https://www.rightmove.co.uk/house-prices.html* search for your own house or your parents, have a look at the price difference over the years. I think you`ll find it interesting.

SEVEN

Getting it right

The perfect Property
Finding the perfect property is easy when you know what you are looking for.

In this chapter we'll look at what my experiences has taught me over the years when trying to find the perfect property. I now work off a simple checklist and unless a property ticks nearly all of my boxes I won't entertain it.

An investment property does not have to tick every point highlighted below, however, the more ticked the more desirable the property will be to prospective tenants.

- **3 bedrooms** (with a minimum of 1 double bedroom) — Families tend to stay longer if they have room to grow in a property and don't have to move due to size. A double bed measures 6ft 3inches long, 4ft 6inch wide — Ideal double room is min. 9ft. x 9ft.

- **2 bedrooms** — (2 doubles) Tenants looking for two-bedroom properties are drawn more towards properties with two good sized double rooms. A single bed measures 6ft 3inches long, 3ft wide – Ideal single room is min. 9ft. x 6ft.

- **Upstairs bathroom** – Tenants tend to prefer not to walk through a kitchen to get to a bathroom and having a bathroom near to bedrooms upstairs is more desirable.

- **Bath and shower combination** – Having a bath and separate shower cubicle is most desirable, an electric shower over a bath is normal and acceptable, however, a bath and no shower or a bath tap with a shower hose is unfavoured by experienced tenants.

- **Small manageable garden or yard** – Tenants are rarely keen gardeners and an investor doesn`t need the hassle of sorting out an overgrown garden at the end of every tenancy. Some gardens prove desirable however it's important that they are easily manageable.

- **Full-sized kitchens are preferred over galley kitchens** – Typically tenants prefer a large kitchen over a galley kitchen (long and thin).

- **No cellar** – Cellars are often damp, cold, wet and typically non-value adding, although not a deal-breaker a cellar is not a major plus for a tenant or an investor.

- **Gas Central heating (GCH)** – GCH with a combi boiler is best. Properties with conventional boilers or storage radiators should be priced to include an upgrade to a more modern system. Electric radiators are expensive and put tenants off rental properties.

- **Double glazed windows & doors** – uPVC windows and doors are best. A property with old wooden or single glazed windows and/or doors should be priced to include an upgrade.

- **Attic rooms** – Although not a deal-breaker an attic room is not as desirable to tenants as a standard bedroom.

- **Leasehold** – It is advisable to only consider apartments with a lease length of more than 150 years and to check the terms of the lease. Leasehold houses are not usually the best investment properties and should be avoided by inexperienced investors if possible.

NB: Mortgage applications become more challenging on properties of non-standard construction (concrete blocks, wooden frame etc.), and/or that are in a poor state of repair (non-functioning bathroom or kitchen, serious damp, pest infestation, subsidence etc.), and/or with Japanese knotweed. Similarly, lenders are less ready to consider mortgages for apartments above shops, freehold apartments, apartments with short leases or very old and listed buildings. As a new investor, these properties are best avoided until you have more experience.

The Perfect Location
An investment area does not have to tick every point below, however, the more ticked the more desirable to prospective tenants the property will be.

- **Avoid main roads** – A property on the main road will typically put a great number of potential tenants off a property and make it increasingly difficult to sell in the future.

- **Parking** - Off-street is preferred, on-street is acceptable, a permit restriction is ok, no parking is a no-deal.

- **Maximum 15-minute walk to a town/city centre** – Convenience is key and being close to the town centre is very desirable for the majority of tenants.

- **Not on a large hill** – tenants tend not to like walking up or parking on large hills. Properties on large hills often see a higher turnover than those on flat ground.

- **Maximum 15-minute walk to a train station** – Ensuring a property is no more than a 15-minute walk to a train station will dramatically increase a tenant pool, especially if it's a mainline station.

- **Maximum 15-minute drive to a motorway** – Having easy and quick road access to a property is another great way to increase a tenant pool.

- **Maximum 15-minute walk to a supermarket** - Convenience sells and being within walking distance to a supermarket will increase longer stays.

- **Close to a primary and secondary school** – Families with young children will be attracted to properties close to schools, this tenant pool tends to stay longer in rental properties.

- **Good local employment** – Large employers bring tenants to an area, a property close to places of work tends to be popular.

The Perfect tenant

It's important to know the tenant type you are ideally wanting to attract when choosing a property.

The below descriptions are general and intended as a guide to help understand the different tenant profiles. Not all tenants are the same and this information is general rather than factual.

Students

Regular student loan payments mean a landlord can rest assured knowing there will always be some money coming in.

There will always be a risk of wild parties, however, a good letting agent who forms a relationship and provides clear expectations can mitigate some of this risk.

- As students are studying, they tend not to want any trouble with a landlord and tend to pay rent without question.
- Due to most students being young and inexperienced with renting they tend to be polite to landlords and letting agents, who they see as a figure of authority.
- Students are often financially dependent on family members and parents are usually willing to act as guarantors.
- Students at universities tend to be intelligent and when problems at a property do arise, they are typically clear, concise and reasonable when asking for issues to be addressed. Parents can become involved with regard to an issue, especially where they are guarantors, and this can usually facilitate matters, rather than causing conflict.
- If a landlord is paying the bills it's worth noting that students are exempt from council tax meaning the landlord would not be required to pay.
- Students want convenience and they will pay for it, they prefer properties that are close to a town centre, their university and a train station.
- If looking to rent to students, it's worth checking the internet strength and speed before buying an investment property.

Young Professionals
Aged approximately 18-29, tenants in this group tend to be single or in a new relationship and value the flexibility of renting. They tend to be optimistic about buying their own home in the future and are in the process of saving for a deposit.

- This group come with a reasonably high turnover as they move on for work, out to live with partners or into their own homes.
- Young professionals tend to be more confident and practical than the student group. If young professionals receive a property in good condition, they tend to return it in good condition and if reported issues are attended to promptly, they tend to look after a property.
- If looking to rent to young professionals, being near to transport links, a town centre and having parking facilities makes a property attractive. This group favour a modern, open, airy and clean place to live.

Young Professional couples

With this group, there is double the security as two separate references can be checked. Also, if anything happens to the employment status of one of the tenants the other can usually cover the rent until another job is secured.

- The professional couple are often good tenants, but career demands often mean they frequently move on.
- Sometimes relationships don't last and tenancies end abruptly.
- Rents are usually paid on time and properties generally looked after.
- As with the young professionals, this group also favour being near to transport links and having parking facilities.
- Young professional couples also like modern, open, airy and clean but are willing to be based further out of a town.

Single parents

Even if rent is subsidised through Housing Benefits, this class of tenant tend to like to be settled and they usually want to keep a property clean and tidy for their children. They are mostly reasonable in requests for repairs or when asking for issues to be resolved.

- Ex and new partners can add risk and with relationship uncertainty, more issues are likely to occur than with other tenant profiles.
- A single parent has experienced life and knows they won't be in a property forever, they can sometimes show this in the way they treat the property.
- This group tends to attract more traffic with family and friends visiting more frequently.
- Due to the costs associated with managing a family as a single parent, there is a heightened risk of rent not being paid.
- This tenant is cost-conscious and will take on properties in less desirable areas and more dated properties than other groups.

Young Families

This group are typically aged between 30-45 they have a greater understanding of the cost involved in purchasing a property and are typically saving for a deposit, renting as a stop-gap between house moves or settling in what they can currently afford due to the costs of running a family.

- If a property is perfect for raising a young family (near to a primary and secondary school, with space for a family to grow, which is clean, modern and safe, with parking, close to the shops and with some open space) then there is a high chance this tenant group will stay long term.
- This group are most likely to ask if they can have pets in the property.
- One if not both of the adults will be working so being close to employers or to transport links will be important.
- The number of bedrooms, size of the kitchen and bathroom and outdoor space matter to this tenant group.

Mature Professionals

This group are typically over the age of 45 and are renting due to a change of circumstances or a lower income. Most do not have children living with them and have less desire to own their own home.

- This group is the "old professionals" they have been through the renting cycle once and for whatever reason, have found themselves back at square one.
- Like the young professionals, they tend to treat a property well.
- Rent is typically paid and they prefer an easy, quiet and hassle-free life.
- This group doesn't care much for outdoor space, they are usually content with a double bedroom and a place to park.

Elderly people

This tenant group tend to be the most pleasant and easy to manage.

Retired people want security, moving home is a big deal and they will do their best to avoid moving around. They know that to get the security they need to pay the rent on time and to treat a property with respect. The elderly also appreciate a long term tenancy so there is no worry of them being evicted with short notice. Typically, at the end of a tenancy, the property is left in good condition.

- Elderly people tend to rarely default on rent, being what we might call 'old fashioned' in this regard.
- They are mostly polite, respectful and reasonable in their requests.
- They tend to be quiet which is especially important if the rental property is a flat or apartment.
- If they like the property they are likely to stay long term.

- The elderly tend to like a small garden, they are not usually a fan of a city location and are often happy with a bus stop close by.

The Perfect Price

Investment properties can work at any price if the numbers stack up, however, my personal sweet spot is between £70,000 - £125,000, let me tell you why.

Properties selling for less than £70,000 run the risk of being located in undesirable areas.
Cheap properties in undesirable areas will cost later down the line.

Undesirable locations attract undesirable tenants and undesirable tenants can cause investors a huge burden with significant cost implications.

Although a cheap property may seem like a great deal on paper when factoring in damage, non-paying tenants and voids, (rooms not occupied by tenants), the return on investment can be dramatically reduced.

Buying on numbers alone can be the biggest and most costly mistake made by new and inexperienced investors.

A property that costs more than £125,000 doesn't usually bring a high return on investment (ROI).

At the time of publication (April 2020) an investor will pay stamp duty on any additional property purchased above £40,000 and once the purchase price exceeds £125,000 the additional percentage due increases from 3% to 5%.

Although some properties do work over the £125,000-mark, rents don't tend to increase in line with the purchase price.

> **Task:** Take a look on Rightmove's websit*e:*
> **https://www.rightmove.co.uk/**
> at properties for sale within a 40-mile radius of your chosen
> area, set the price range to a maximum of £70,000 and have
> a look into the areas that the properties are located.

Properties priced below £70,000 or above £125,000 can and do
work as investment properties. My personal spot is simply a
guide to help mitigate as much risk as possible for new and
inexperienced investors.

Identifying a property hot spot
It's important to assess which properties to buy, specifically
selecting the property type, location and tenant profile.

To increase the desirability and to help minimise void periods (a
time when the property is vacant between tenant) selecting an
area with a large supply of the chosen tenant profile is
advisable.

Investing in an up-and-coming property hotspot will ensure
demand and offer the best chance of capital appreciation (the
property price going up in value).

To identify an up-and-coming hot spot lookout for the factors
below:
- **Major regeneration projects -** Are there any plans to
  develop the area or a specific area within a patch, has a
  budget been allocated for infrastructure upgrades?
- **Transport link change or development -** Are there any
  plans to build new major roads, is a direct train line
  being added?
- **Wholesale food outlets -** Supermarkets spend millions
  researching population growth. If there are several
  shopping centres or supermarkets due to open in an
  area the chances are the population is on the up.

- **New schools** - New schools prove population growth and almost guarantee an influx of young families.

Does the layout of a property matter?

Being picky about a property will ensure the product is always desirable.

Here are some example floor plans of both 2 and 3-bed properties. These examples take full advantage of the floor space, have good room sizes and a desirably located bathroom. These layouts tend to be very attractive to most tenants.

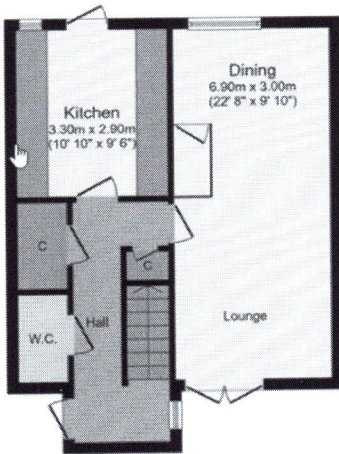

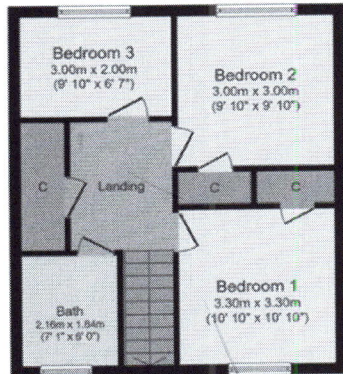

LOUNGE
4.5m x 3.6m
14'8 x 11'11

KITCHEN
3.0m x 1.7m
9'9 x 5'7

HALL

BEDROOM
3.7m x 2.7m
12'1 x 8'10

BATHROOM
2.0m x 1.7m
6'5 x 5'6

LANDING

BEDROOM
3.7m x 2.7m
12'1 x 8'10

Bedroom 2

Bathroom

Master
Bedroom

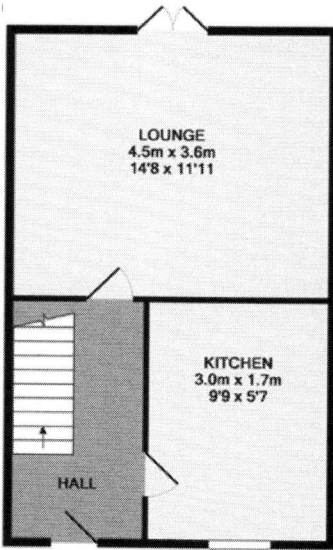

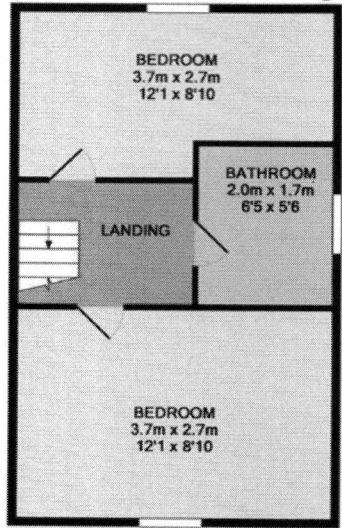

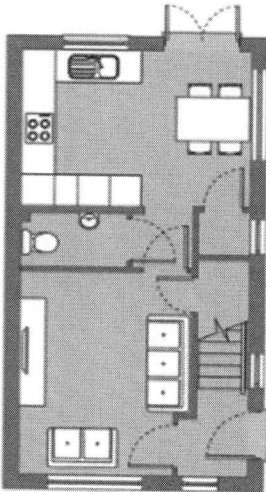

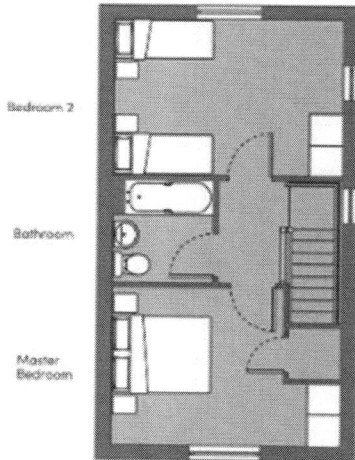

Task: Spend some time on Rightmove's website looking at floor plans in your area. You will often find that properties in a selected price bracket and area are consistent in their layout. Find the ideal 2- and 3-bedroom floor plan that you believe to be the best set up for an investment property within your patch.

Investing from a distance

When managing a property from a distance the property age, specification and condition should be seriously consicered. Maintenance issues and renovations are more difficult to plan and manage from a distance.

When managing from afar, it could be worth considering new or nearly new properties (including apartments) as these property types tend to require less maintenance. Although it will often be more challenging to find a great deal when considering newer builds.

Having a reliable and trustworthy power team in place to help ensure a property remains hands-off and hassle-free is funda-mental in managing from a distance.

In the next chapter, we will look into power teams.

Task: Before you move on, make a list of professionals who you think you will need to form part of your power team.

EIGHT

It's all about the power team

Having a team of professionals take care of the day to day tasks will help with systemisation, scaling and the amount of involvement required from an investor. Time is money in today's world and a savvy investor will consider the value of their own time when a job needs doing.

No investor will be an expert in every area so working with industry professionals will ensure a business runs smoothly.

Recommendations are generally the best way to find trusted and reliable power team candidates. It's advisable to trial professionals until a trustworthy expert is found. Although it's far easier to settle with an average service taking the time to build a team of exceptional individuals could be the difference between being successful and highly successful.

Below is a suggested list of team members who could form part of a property investor's power team.

Estate agents

Having a strong relationship with local estate agents can increase the chances of being presented with great deals even before they hit the open market. Estate agents have the job of selling properties and if they know, trust and favour an investor, they are more likely to get in contact when that perfect property hits their desk.

Property specialist accountant

An accountant is there to manage, advise, assist and ensure tax-efficiency. Mainstream accountants tend not to be specialists in property and could fall short of the hints and tips that are known by those experienced in the industry.

Investment specialist, all market, independent mortgage advisor

A family friend, dad's mate or a broker who sorted the residential mortgage isn't usually the best professional to call upon when it comes to 'buy to let' investment mortgages. Having a trustworthy, down to earth, creative, all market, independent mortgage advisor who speaks openly and honestly with clients on the team will put an investor in a great position when looking to build a property portfolio.

Mentor, friend or buddy

Property investing can be a lonely place, being surrounded with positive, knowledgeable and experienced investors can help motivate and keep a newbie on track. A great way to meet like-minded individuals is to join some of the many Facebook groups out there that are full of property enthusiasts. Some of the best and most popular are at the time of publication are:

- Property Newbies
- UK Property Traders
- All About Property

Property investment specialist solicitor
When selecting a solicitor, it's important to find someone who is able to communicate in laymen's terms. Solicitors have a reputation of being slow, unresponsive and uninformative. Spending some time finding a top-notch solicitor will save time and reduce stress levels after an offer has been accepted.

RICS surveyor
Having an RICS, (Royal Institute of Chartered Surveyors) surveyor that offers all surveys and a valuation, who can act quickly and report back in a timely manner is very handy to have on the team.

Insurance broker
Insurance policies can be very confusing, often jargon-filled and small print heavy. Having a property specialist insurance broker to explain the documents, wording and language can save wasting money on a policy that won't pay-out.

Letting agent
Finding the perfect letting agent to work with is up there on the "most important" list when it comes to setting up a property letting business. The decision of which agent to work with can be the difference between a hassle-free hands-off investment and a huge hands-on headache.

Time spent finding an agent that not only excels in their field but also who compliments an investor's working and management style will be well worth it.

A professionally set up letting agent should have a team of contractors who they can call upon to have specific property issues sorted. However, there is value for an investor in building their own team and passing on vetted contacts to the chosen letting agent.

By handpicking a team, the managing of the business is not left to chance, with a full team in place to maintain every element of the property portfolio an investor will have the control they need without the need to do the job themselves.

Handyman/woman

A reliable and trustworthy right-hand man/woman will help make life easy. A jack of all trades who can sort small simple issues will ensure properties stay fit for purpose. It's advisable for the handyperson to assist with initially preparing of a property to give them a feel for the place. Once they become comfortable, they will be able to maintain the property moving forward.

Plumber/gas engineer

A plumber is the most commonly called upon tradesperson. Gas, boilers, sinks, taps, baths, and radiators: where there is water or gas, a plumber will be involved. Annual landlord gas certificates can be managed by a plumber and if fully systemised a plumber can contact a letting agent or vice versa to gain access when a gas check is due.

A great plumber who knows the properties within a portfolio well can save an investor hundreds of pounds on unnecessary callouts from tenants when simple instructions can be passed over a phone.

It's advisable to find a gas engineer from recommendations and to keep trialling until the perfect match is found. If treated well and looked after, a gas engineer can become an investor's eyes and ears on the ground and even report back on the performance of the letting agents.

Electrician

Electrical certificates, extractor fans, lights, cookers, ovens, boilers, thermostats there are several areas for a sparky to manage within an investment property.

Having an electrician who knows their way around will always help.

Plasterer
This trade is not cheap, and quality plastering comes at a cost. A skilled plasterer is a team member who will be frequently called upon while building your portfolio. A skilled, clean and tidy plasterer is worth their weight in gold. It's not advisable to skimp and save on this one or it will cost in the long run.

Roofing specialist
Roofing jobs require trust. It's advisable to choose a roofer wisely as jobs tend to be expensive and results are hard to view. Expectations can be set during initial conversations by asking for before and after photos of the work carried out.

Carpet fitter
Carpets, vinyl and flooring will always need replacing, using the same carpet fitter will allow an investor to order and action from a distance with confidence. By using someone independent and local there will be a higher chance of getting access to off cut deals, more honest and open advice and added transparency on jobs.

Glazier
Doors and windows are not cheap, having a trustworthy glazier who can be called on to assess and update windows and doors, add trickle vents and replace blown panes is always a great contact to have.

Property photographer
Any letting agent should take photos of a property for advertising purposes. However, an expert in lettings is rarely also a pro photographer. Some agents outsource to a professional photographer however it's common for one of the office staff to simply pop round to the property with a smart phone.

> ***Task:*** Take a look at the 'To Rent' tab on Rightmove and notice which of the properties instantly grab your attention, typically it`s the ones with great photos.

Personally, I have a professional photographer on my power team and before a new property is let I have photos taken. I pay £95 for over 20 edited, high-quality shots and then pass them to my letting agent. My agent uses these photos every time there is a tenant turnover and I can be confident that when notice is given my agent is armed with high-quality photos and can relist the property instantly.

Council representative
Although being on friendly first name terms with a contact at the local council isn't a necessity it can only be of benefit if an investor is planning to build a sizable portfolio. A great way to get a contact name is to give the local licensing department a call and to ask if there are any rules or legislation to be aware of before buying in the area.

NINE

Adding value to create wealth

Buy, Refurbish, Rent, Refinance (BRRR)
This strategy is popular with investors who live close to their investment property and have some DIY/renovation experience and skills. It is often sold as the dream strategy implying that an investor can easily recycle their money and build a portfolio on one deposit alone.

Although it is possible to release equity from a deal, securing a deal where the entire deposit and cost of the refurbishment can be released is not easy to find.

The strategy involves purchasing a property that needs attention or where it's possible to add value. Once purchased the property is renovated, updated and modernised before renting it out. When work has been completed an investor re-finances (re-mortgages) the property and releases equity. The equity is created by increasing the value of the property with the work that has been carried out.

Often overlooked by inexperienced investors is the timeframe in which you can re-finance after the purchase. Most mortgage lenders have a minimum of 2 years before you can re-finance without paying a penalty. Re-financing before the fixed time is seen as unfavourable with lenders and could affect lendability in the future.

Another option is to use bridging finance, this is a short-term finance solution where the loan is paid off after work is completed and the property is mortgaged. However, bridging finance comes at a much higher cost than a standard mortgage and if a project takes longer than expected the interest rates increase dramatically, bridging isn't advisable for first-time investors.

This strategy is increasingly difficult to execute when managed at a distance due to the increased costs of tradespeople and the distance management aspect.

Let`s look at an example
Purchase price £75,000. (A)

Deposit £18,750 (75% Loan to value, interest-only mortgage). (B)

Mortgage (amount borrowed) £56,250. (C)

Renovation costs £7,000. (D)

Total cost to investor (B+D) £25,750.

New value on re-financing £120,000. (E)

New deposit = 25% of (E) = £30,000 (F)

Mortgage on (E) = £90,000. (G)

The previous mortgage (C) will need to be paid off with the new loan. (E)

New mortgage (G) - previous mortgage (C) = £33,750.

However, there is already £25,750 (B) + (D) in the property. £30,000 (F) - £25,750 (B+D) = £4,250 (H) required to top up deposit.

£33,750 (difference between previous and new mortgage) - £4,250 (H) = £29,500 (equity to be released).

In this example, the investor initially put £25,750 (B+D) into the deal and then after the renovation took out £29,500 meaning the entire initial investment was released + £3,750.

By combining inflation, leverage, time and by adding value to a property it is possible to create long term wealth.

Here is a case study of one of my own properties.

This property was purchased in 2016, it required a full renovation, new kitchen, bathroom, boiler, heating system anc complete redecoration. Checkout the photos followed by the numbers.

Purchase Price: (2016) £105,000	Revaluation: (2019) £145,000
Deposit: £26,250	Equity Release £29,128
Renovation: £7,860	
Other Costs: £1,268	Capital Left In Deal: £6,250
Total Cash Invested: £35,378	
Rental Income: £725 PCM	Net Monthly Income:
Return On Investment: 12.4%	£459.25

To re-finance a property an investor simply waits until the initial fixed term is up on the original mortgage and then usually with the assistance of a mortgage broker, switches the property onto a new fixed-term mortgage product.

The equity in the property is returned to the investor tax-free.

Top Tip: Adding value can be as simple as decorating a dated property, however, the most value is created when rooms are added or an issue that would put off other buyers off is fixed.

In 2013 I purchased a 2-bed terrace house for £89,000. The property had a 16ft. front bedroom and 2 windows, on the next page is the property floor plan.

2 bedroom terraced house

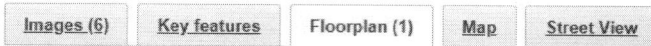

Images (6) | Key features | Floorplan (1) | Map | Street View

Master Floorplan Image

When renovating the property, I added a stud wall creating two bedrooms in the front room (see above), when the property was refinanced in 2019 it was valued at £140,000.

Task: Have a look at 2-bed properties in your chosen area to see if you can find a floor plan that would allow you to add another room. Remember you want any room to be big enough for a single bed, a wardrobe and chest of draws as a minimum.

TEN

Actual values

True market value

Don`t be fooled by a high asking or guide price. Estate agents and sellers often list properties at higher prices than the amount they are willing to accept. This technique is frequently used as it is common for buyers to negotiate on advertised prices.

It's important to remember that the advertised price of a property isn't necessarily the actual market value.

Task: Follow the next steps to calculate the true market value of a property. It is advisable to identify 3-5 properties with the same specification (room count, floor plan, garden size, condition, parking, location) as the property being analysed. The comparable properties should be in close proximity to the property being researched.

---

1. Head over to Google and search Rightmove sold prices.

2. Type in the street, city, county and first three characters of the postcode of the property you are analysing and run in list view.

3. You should set your filters to
   - Within ¼ of a mile.
   - Sold in the last 1 year.
   - Property type to match the property you are analysing.
   - If the property is freehold or leasehold.

4. You can then sort by address, date sold or price.

The list will now be shown in alphabetical order making it simple to check if other properties have sold on the same street as the property being analysed. It's advisable to find 3-5 properties that are of the same specification as the property being analysed.

5. Once the 3-5 comparable properties have been decided on, adding the sold prices together and then dividing the total by the number of comparable properties gives the true market value of the property being analysed.

This is the method used by surveyors to calculate the value of a property they are analysing.

Is the asking price the same as the true market value for the property you have analysed?

True rental value
Knowing the true rental value will ensure your numbers are accurate.

> **Task:** Work out the actual rental value of a property you are interested in. Follow the steps below to find 3-5 sim lar properties with the same specification (room count, floor plan, garden size, condition, parking, location) as the property you are analysing. The comparable properties need be in close proximity to the property you are researching.

1. Visit the 'Open Rent' website - www.openrent.co.uk

2. Type the chosen area into the search bar.

3. Set your search area distance to 1 KM.

4. Properties for let with the advertised price will be presented.

5. A search can be refined further by using the filters.

6. At the foot of the page properties that have a ready been let are listed, by clicking the advert the agreed let price is shown.

7. It`s advisable to compare 3-5 properties to ensure accuracy when calculating the true rental value.

The Rightmove website can also be used to view similar properties in the area and for what they are being advertised.

On Rightmove, the properties have not yet had a let agreed so the results should only be used as a guide.

1. Visit the Rightmove website.

2. Type the chosen area into the search bar.

3. Select 'To rent'.

4. Filter to match the chosen property.
5. Select 'Include Let Agreed' properties.

6. By selecting Map view, properties to let in the area are displayed.

7. Hovering over a property in Map view presents a property summary. Selecting 'See full property details' is an efficient way to check if a property matches the property being analysed.

8. It's advisable to compare 3-5 properties for the best indication of what other investors are asking for their properties.

Please remember that, on Rightmove, the properties you are viewing are not necessarily the rental amount the property has achieved they are advertised prices only.

Was your rental estimation the same as the true rental value for the property you have analysed?

ELEVEN

The Numbers

Gross yield
Gross yield is commonly used by sellers but why?

Gross yield is often presented by the seller of a property because the numbers look as good as they possibly can do.

But because gross yield doesn't factor in any expenses or costs, it means that the calculation is a very loose way of assessing a property.

Estate agents and deal sourcers typically use gross yield as the calculation works in their favour.

The calculation
Annual rental income divided by property purchase price then multiplied by 100 = Gross yield.

Example
Monthly rental income £600 x 12 = Annual rental income = £7,200.

Annual rental income £7,200 divided by property purchase price £100,000 = 0.072.

0.072 multiplied by 100 = 7.2% gross yield.

£600 x 12 = £7200 / £100,000 = 0.072 x 100 = 7.2% gross yield.

> **Task:** Choose a property to analyse in this chapter and use the calculation above to work out the gross yield.

Net yield

Net yield is a more accurate calculation than gross yield as expenses and costs are deducted (i.e. management fees, mortgage repayment, maintenance, insurance, service charge etc.). However, the net yield calculation factors in borrowed money and looks at the deal as a whole rather than calculating the actual personal money invested.

The calculation

Annual rental income minus annual expenses divided by property purchase cost then multiplied by 100 = Net yield.

Example

Monthly rental income £600 x 12 = Annual rental income = £7,200.

Annual rental income £7,200 minus expenses £4,800 = Annual net profit £2,400.

Annual net profit £2,400 divided by property purchase price £100,000 = 0.024.

0.024 multiplied by 100 = 2.4% Net yield.

£600 x 12 = £7200 - £4800 = £2400 / £100,000 = 0.024 x 100 = 2.4%.

> **Task:** Using the calculation above workout the net yield on the property you selected in the previous task.

Return on investment (ROI)

ROI is a far more accurate calculation that works on the actual money that an investor puts into a deal. The borrowed money is set aside, however, the cost of borrowing the loan is factored in.

The Calculation

Annual rental income minus expenses divided by total investment then multiplied by 100 = ROI.

Example

Monthly rental income £600 x 12 = Annual rental income = £7,200.

Annual rental income £7,200 minus expenses £4,800 = Annual net profit £2,400.

Annual net profit £2,400 divided by total investment £25,000 = 0.096.

0.096 multiplied by 100 = 9.6% ROI.

£600 x 12 = £7,200 - £4,800 = £2,400 / £25,000 = 0.096 x 100 = 9.6%.

The above calculations can be worked out with varying numbers depending on exactly what expenses are factored into the equation. On the following page is a list of costs associated with purchasing a 'buy to let' investment property. N.B. These costs are not always considered when a deal is presented.

- Renovations and maintenance including boiler service/checks.
- Accountancy fees.
- Mortgage repayments.
- Insurance.

- Ground rent & service charge (if applicable).
- Gas, electric, council tax, wifi, water, TV licence.
- Letting agent fees.
- Mortgage set up, broker fee, valuation fee.
- Surveys.
- Tenant set up fee.
- Sourcing fee.
- Furniture.
- Legal fee, solicitor costs.

Task: Using the return on investment calculation, work out the ROI on the property you have selected to analyse.

Additional rate stamp duty
(At the time of publication April 2020)
In April 2016 a higher rate stamp duty came into effect. This means anyone purchasing an additional property will be subject to paying a higher rate of stamp duty land tax (SDLT) on top of the purchase price of a property.

Properties purchased for less than £40,000 are not subject to any stamp duty.

If a property purchase price is between £40,000 and £125,000 an additional 3% SDLT is payable on the full amount.

If the purchase price is between £125,000 and £250,000 an extra 5% is payable on the amount above £125,000 and 3% on the amount below £125,000.

The additional rate also applies to properties purchased within a limited company.

A common scenario is an investor buying a property for a child to live in whilst at university. If the investor has a residential property and purchases a property for their child there will be additional stamp duty to pay. However, if the property was purchased in the child's name and the child didn't own another property there would be no additional stamp duty to pay.

Couples who are married or in a civil partnership will be subject to the higher rate stamp duty if they purchase an additional property.

If a property is owned abroad and an additional property is purchased in the UK, the additional rate of stamp duty will apply.

Commercial properties, however, are exempt from the additional stamp duty and this also applies to mixed-use properties such as shops with apartments above.

The deal calculator
Knowing how to work out what's a good deal and what's not when it comes to property investing is vital. Although every investor will have a personal goal, being crystal clear on the numbers is imperative when analysing a deal. Getting the numbers wrong could be a very costly mistake and one that all investors should avoid.

All 'new2property' clients are issued with a comprehensive deal calculator which will break down and analyse any 'buy to let' investment property. As a reader of this book, you too can have access to this amazing tool.

Download the 'new2property' Deal Calculator using this address
https://www.new2property.co.uk/deal-calculator-download
I'll also send you a link to a video tutorial to ensure you get the best out of the tool.

Task: Using a property that you have been analysing, input the numbers into the deal calculator. Does it stack up as you thought it might?

Top Tip: When a deal doesn't stack up change the purchase price until the numbers work for you, then you know exactly what price you can pay for the property when the negotiations begin.

Accounting for investors
Failing to claim for the small things will cost you big in the long term.

If a limited company is the best set up for an investor, a limited company bank account will be required. All transactions related to a property business should run through a limited company account.

If an investor chooses to buy in their own name using a separate bank account is advisable. All property income and expense should be kept separate from personal monies. Ensuring accounts are kept clean, tidy and easy to manage will help an investor and an accountant. Separating a property business from day to day spending allows an investor to track profit and loss, ensuring investments are profiting.

Expenses can be deducted to calculate a taxable rental profit. Expenses must be wholly and exclusively for the purposes of renting out the property.

What can you claim for?
- General maintenance and repairs to the property, but not improvements (such as replacing a laminate kitchen worktop with a granite worktop).
- Water rates, council tax, gas and electricity.

- Financial costs such as bank charges or insurance, such as landlords' and contents.
- Costs of services, including the wages of gardeners and cleaners.
- Letting agent fees and management fees.
- Legal fees for lets of a year or less, or for renewing a lease for less than 50 years.
- Accountant's fees.
- Rents, ground rents and service charges.
- Vehicle running costs (only the proportion used for your rental business) and travel, for example, fuel, parking, train or bus fares.
- Training related to your business, for example, the cost of this online course.
- Advertising or marketing, for example, website costs and advertising for new tenants.
- Office costs, for example, stationery or phone bills.

What can't you claim for?

- The full amount of your mortgage payment - only the interest element of your mortgage payment can be offset against your income. Unless your property is owned in a limited company.
- Private telephone calls - you can only claim for the cost of calls relating to your property rental business.
- Clothing - for example, if you bought a suit to wear to a meeting relating to your property rental business, you can't claim for the cost as wearing the suit is partly for your rental business and partly to keep you warm - no identifiable part is for your property rental business.
- Personal expenses - you can't claim for any expense that was not incurred solely for your property rental business.

Your accountant will manage what goes where. Your job is simply to keep clean and tidy records for your accountant to work with.

Task: Add the cost of this book to the 'new2property' deal calculator spreadsheet as well as any other costs you have incurred to date relating to your property business.

Top Tip: Checking bank statements against recorded accounting monthly will ensure books are in good order when the end of the year comes.

TWELVE

Using Rightmove like the pros

Follow the steps below to discover how the pros use Rightmove

1. Visit Rightmove's website.

2. Create an account.

3. Type in a chosen location.

4. Set the filters, this will help drill down to a selected property type.
- Search radius.
- Price range.
- No. of bedrooms.
- Property type.

5. Select 'Find properties'.

6. Clicking the bell icon creates a notification for your search which can be set up to be emailed to you either instantly, daily, every 3 days or every 7 days. It's worth noting that multiple searches can be set up. Setting up

alerts will save you time scrolling through pages of properties and ensure you get notified of properties of interest.

7. Results can be viewed in a list or on a map.

8. Specific search areas can be selected by clicking 'Edit search area'.

9. In the 'Edit search area' window you can create a specific search area by moving the boxes on the map.

10. When you have highlighted your area of interest, select 'View Properties'.

11. Properties matching the set criteria will be presented in the highlighted area.

12. Clicking on the red dots will present an overview of the selected property.

13. When a property of interest is found, select 'See full property details' and you will be presented with the full property advert.

14. On each property advert, there is the option to select 'market info'.

15. Selecting 'market info' will present information direct from the land registry on when the property has sold in the past and for how much.

16. By selecting 'Map & Street View' you can view the street in picture form, which is a great way to get a feel for an area and to check what's around a chosen property.

17. Selecting 'market info' followed by 'sold' will present similar properties that have sold nearby. This information is direct from the land registry and is useful to help with true market value research.

18. If looking for projects or specific types of properties such as HMOs, (house of multiple occupancy), there is a keyword search tool that will allow a more refined search. Head back to the main list of your search and click 'Add keywords' at the top of the screen next to 'Prioritise properties with'...

19. Selecting 'My Rightmove' on the main menu bar followed by 'investor news' allows users to set up monthly updates on trends and statistics on a chosen area.

20. Housing trends can also be an interesting read and can be viewed by clicking 'inspire' on the main menu bar followed by 'housing trends'.

21. By adding the property log extension to a Google Chrome browser any price changes to a property are automatically displayed on a listing. This tool gives a great insight into the sale history of any property. Simply google 'property log' and add the extension to get started.

To watch a video tutorial on how to use Rightmove like the pros head over to the new2property You Tube channel and search "How to use Rightmove like the pros"

THIRTEEN

Get on the agent's hot buyer list

It's common to hear that investors have been advised not to trust estate agents and how they often go out of their way to avoid contact.

A savvy investor will leverage an estate agent's skills, knowledge and time. By looking after the local agents and treating them well an investor can effectively utilise their skills as a professional property sourcer.

> *Myth buster:* An estate agent's motivation doesn't come from squeezing every last pound out of a sale: it comes from selling properties.

What does an estate agent have to offer?
- An estate agent has properties to sell.
- They get paid for selling property, so they are driven and motivated to sell.

- Most people who have a property to sell go to an estate agent.
- An estate agent's job requires them to be experts in the local area.
- They commonly have information on rentability and rental value.

How can an estate agent help an investor?

- An estate agent can be leveraged to help search for properties.
- They can target specific properties with set criteria in mind.
- An agent has information on properties before they hit the open market.
- They know why a vendor (the person selling the property), wants to sell and how likely they are to take a lower offer.
- It's their job to find buyers properties.
- They can negotiate on an investor's behalf and push a sale through.
- Once an offer is accepted, they should manage the sale through to completion.

Top tips on working with an estate agent

- Be nice and polite.
- Be friendly and reliable.
- Be serious and don't let them down.
- Act quickly and professionally.
- Be clear on your criteria.
- Have a deposit and an AIP (agreement in principle) ready.
- Always provide detailed feedback after viewings.

An efficient way to make initial contact with local estate agents is to drop them a group email. A list of estate agents in a particular area can be obtained by simply Googling estate

HOW TO BUY TO LET

agents and the name of the area being searched. Some companies will have direct email addresses and others a contact form for enquiries.

Although it takes some time to extract the individual company email addresses it's a worthy task. Using a template email is an efficient way of contacting a high number of estate agents in one hit. The 'new2property' Deal Calculator can be used to collate contact information and once compiled, a blanket email can be sent to all companies using the 'Bcc function' on an email.

On the Zoopla website, it is also possible to run a list of all agents in a local area and to send out one email template. Although this could save some time, the list isn't always 100% accurate, so it's worth cross-referencing the list with a manual Google search.

The template can also be dropped into any contact forms. Here is an example template email.

Good afternoon,

I hope you are well,

My name is XXXX and I'm hoping you can help me,

I'm looking to purchase approximately 3 properties over the next year that match the criteria
below:
- 3 bedrooms
- Min. 1 double bedroom
- Single rooms must be large enough for a single bed, wardrobe and set of drawers
- Easy to maintain/small garden or yard
- No cellar

- Within a 15 min walk of the town centre
- Within a 15 min walk of the train station
- Within a 15 min walk of a primary school
- Listed price between £70,000 - £125,000
- uPVC windows and doors or priced to upgrade
- GCH or priced to upgrade
- Renovation work is ok, however, must be reflected in the price

I am an investor and will be buying the properties for investment purposes, I have an AIP and proof of deposit ready to present. I don`t have anything to sell and I`m not part of a chain, I can move as quickly as a vendor wishes.

Please feel free to add me to your database, I am happy to receive calls during the day and can view at short notice. The best number to reach me on is XXXXXXX

When I am next passing your office, I will call in and introduce myself.

I would really appreciate if you could give me a heads up on any properties that fall on your desk that fit the above criteria.

Have a great day, I`ll look forward to hearing from you.

Kind regards

If the estate agent being contacted also has a letting agent this is a great opportunity to ask for information on the service they offer and the commission they charge.

When the estate agents reply, it's good practice to update the email address and contact name on your spreadsheet to ensure a more personal email can be sent moving forward.

A decent estate agent can be a fundamental part of any investor's power team; it's important not to miss the opportunity to leverage their knowledge and skills.

Task: Send a group email to all estate agents in your area and start to build your contact list on the 'new2property' Deal Calculator spreadsheet.

FOURTEEN

Viewing

When viewing properties, I strongly suggest looking for problems and issues. It's advisable to take photos and to spend time collating clear and detailed notes when in a property. This information will be required when submitting an offer. Having a strong, detailed and accurate offer can save thousands of pounds.

Top Tip: View in twos: one to chat with the agent to stop them from distracting the person viewing and the other to go through the property with a fine-tooth comb.

The most expensive elements within a property are the parts where a thorough check is needed.

- Windows and doors - UPVC, age, do they open and close smoothly and are there any clouded panes?
- Roof - age, condition, any dipping, missing tiles etc?
- Boiler - age, type, condition?
- Kitchen - cooker, oven, integrated fridge freezer; is it modern and attractive or will it need replacing?

- Bathroom - shower, is it electric or does it run off the taps; is the bathroom modern or will it need replacing?
- Electrics - age of fuse box, metal or plastic casing?
- Walls - If you remove the wallpaper is there a chance the plaster may come off?
- Damp - Are there any signs of damp anywhere in the property?

When viewing properties, it's wise to take the items below:

- A small, light ladder to check the loft.
- A torch to check dark places or any rooms where lights don't work.
- The 'new2property' viewing checklist to record your findings.
- A damp meter to check the moisture levels on walls.
- A camera for evidence to back up your offer.
- Binoculars to view the roof.

> Task: Checkout the 'new2property' viewing checklist here:
> ***https://www.new2property.co.uk/free-viewing-checklist***
> and then head out to view a property as a practice.

FIFTEEN

How to best offer and negotiate

I f done right this step could save you thousands.

Now you are a pro on the 'new2property' Deal Calculator you're able to, efficiently and accurately, work out how much you can pay for a property to make the deal work.

Before offering, it`s advisable to have the below information to hand.

- The price the property was last purchased for and when.
- The true market value of the property.
- The possible rent achievable.
- The amount that can be paid for the property to achieve the desired ROI.
- Any issues or work required to get the property to a lettable condition.

> **Top Tip:** Write down a top-line figure that you are prepared to pay for the property and keep this to hand when you begin negotiating.

Staying cool, calm and calculated with the numbers will help to stop emotions taking over and keep an investor from overpaying for the property.

Photos should have been taken when the initial viewing took place, all problems and issues should have been recorded and this information will be required for the initial offer.

Sending an offer email is a good way to help secure a property for a great price. This technique has been known to save thousands of pounds if everything falls into place.
It's important for an investor to come across to the estate agent as professional, knowledgeable and a strong prospective buyer. Having the agent onside to negotiate and to push for an offer to be accepted is imperative in getting a low offer accepted.

> **Top Tip:** If your first offer is accepted, it's a common belief that you have offered too high. Some say that unless you are embarrassed about your first offer then it shouldn't be submitted. You should offer low enough for the first amount to be rejected, this will allow you to gain further information from the seller.

Offering a non-rounded amount, for example, £71,250 rather than £70,000 is a technique used by investors to imply they have a full and accurate understanding of the property's value even if they don't. Statistics show that there is a higher success rate on non-rounded offer being accepted for properties and other assets.

An offer should be approximately an equal amount lower than the asking price is higher to the desired purchase price. For example, if the property is listed at £110,000 and for the deal to work, the purchase price needs to be £100,000 the starting offer should be £90,000. Whilst negotiating offers will go up from £90,000 to a max of £100,000 with the aim being for the vendor to come down from £110,000 to £100,000.

Within an offer email, reasons for the reduced amount should be highlighted. The idea is to provide the estate agent with ammunition to help persuade the vendor to sell at a lower price. Offering low with no explanation is a common mistake made by investors.

As well as a list of faults/costs it`s worth highlighting at least three cheaper comparable properties in the area to give weight to an offer. The idea is to prove that properties in the same area are selling for less than the property is being advertised for. It`s important to only highlight properties with the same specification and on similar streets as close to the property being offered on as possible. If cheaper properties cannot be found in the area then this section should be left out.

Researching the area and looking for anything that could help build a case as to why the property is worth less can help with securing a lower price. Are there any major works planned nearby? Are any local employers moving on? Is the area populated by only one nationality? Anything concrete can be used to give reasons why other buyers may not be interested in the property.

Within the offer email all issues discovered when viewing should be highlighted with an estimate of the cost to rectify the problem.

Attaching photographic evidence with reference to the photos is a great way to emphasise the highlighted issues.

Here is an example offer email:

---

103 Example Street, Nottingham, NG3 4SQ

Hi David,

I hope you are well,

Firstly, I'd like to thank you for organising the viewing at 103 Example Street, it was great to meet you and I very much appreciate you showing me around and explaining the property history.

I wasn't shocked by the overall condition of the property, however, there is more work required than I was expecting. When considering the issues that need attention the numbers don't quite stack up for me at the moment.

I would really like to purchase the property however for me to be able to make it work as an investment property I will need a reduction in the advertised price.

I've highlighted some points below that I was hoping you could use to help me negotiate with the vendor?

- Bathroom radiator showing signs of rust – will need replacing £150 – photo number 1.
- Entrance concrete step cracked, and slab lose – will need re-concreting £100 – photo number 2
- Garden fence very old, worn and broken in 3 parts – 4 new panels needed £80 – photo number 3
- Shower screen is damaged and hanging off bottom hinge – will need replacing £150 – photo number 4
- Carpets throughout are heavily worn – will need replacing £1700 – photo number 5
- Window in the back bedroom does not open – possibly need new window £600 – photo number 6

- Back door has dropped, and the seal is heavily worn — will need a service £150
- Kitchen window seal has blown — pane needs replacing £250 – photo number 7
- There are no air vents in the lounge chimney – vent needs creating £1500 – photo number 8
- Kitchen is very dated and will need modernising - £4500 – photo number 9

I know you will be aware this property will only be attractive to investors as the location is not desirable for first-time buyers. Also, for an investor, the additional home stamp duty puts the purchase price up by 3%; the vendors might not be aware of this.

A student let model on this property would not be advisable due to it being a 3 bed in an Article 4 area, meaning it's not possible to let the property to more than 2 students. The student market is also far from buoyant at the moment whilst the property is quite a distance out of town and too close to the football stadium to attract the student profile.

There are also major works scheduled to take place within the next few years when the football stadium will be moved. This will, of course, cause disruption to anyone residing in the area making the property undesirable to some tenants.

With the UK recently leaving the EU there is a reduction in the foreign community in Nottingham. Finding tenants for this property won't be as easy as it once was, knowing that this area is heavily populated with Eastern European tenants. I am aware this possible decrease in population is putting off a number of investors.

I have run some comparisons on properties close by, with three beds and that have sold in the last year. My findings can be seen below:

- 82 Sincil Bank, 3 bed, £85k, 30 June 2019
- 97 Portland St, 3 bed £81k, 19 May 2019
- 47 Pennell St, 3 bed, £83k, 11 Jan 2019

With the above in mind, I would like to run the offer of £81,250 by you. I don't want to offend anyone so let me know your thoughts.

I will be purchasing in my limited company's name, I do not have anything to sell. I have a proof of deposit and a mortgage agreement in principle. I am a committed investor and can move as quickly as the vendor would like.

Thanks again for showing me around, I'll look forward to hearing from you

Kind regards

NB: Article 4 was mentioned in the letter which relates to HMO and house share strategies. For further information about Article 4 head over to the new2property You Tube channel and search "HMO, multi let, house share, article 4"

Emphasising being in a strong buying position will give a vendor confidence to proceed. In the UK it's very easy to pull out of an agreed sale and statistics show that approximately 30% of all agreed sales fall through. Being a safe bet will play in an investor's favour.

Nine out of ten times the estate agent will go ahead and submit the offer on receipt of the email. They may come back and ask if they are to make the offer official.

> **Top Tip:** An estate agent can have a strong influence on a seller. To get a good deal it's important to have an estate agent pushing for an offer to be accepted. Rapport and relationship building are paramount at this stage.

> **Task:** Now it's time for you to construct an offer email to send to the estate agent. Download the email template *here:* **https://www.new2property.co.uk/offer-letter-template**

After an initial offer has been submitted it's expected that the estate agent will come back with a rejected offer, this is where the previously formed relationship should be utilised to get further information on the vendor's thoughts and what price they are prepared to accept. It's important to ask directly and to push if necessary, for the amount the vendor is willing to accept.

Once the lower amount is confirmed it can be assumed as a revised asking price.

Some agents are better than others at holding their tongue, however, it's usually possible to break them down if a strong relationship has been previously formed. If a counteroffer is presented it can also be used as the new asking price and negotiated lower.

The aim is to have an offer agreed no higher than the initial amount written down at the beginning of this chapter.

When going back with a second and third offer it's advisable to leave sometime between the offers. I'll explain why below.

Please bear in mind with this technique you always risk losing the property to another buyer.

> **Task:** Think about the emotion the seller will be experiencing when selling a property.

Offer 1 submitted - Excited, the possibility of selling and moving on, no more hassle with the property, feeling optimistic.

Offer 1 received - Disappointment - not the offer expected, not moving anymore, stuck with the property, feeling disappointed.

By leaving time at this point (2/3 days) the seller will question if their price is right, they will start to think about ways they could drop the price and make it work, they'll be thinking what if no one else offers and they get stuck with the property, what if they are asking too much? They will start to experience doubt.

The second offer should be one offer away from the final amount and approximately halfway between offer number one and the ideal purchase price. The third and final offer should be the ideal purchase price.

Offer 2 submitted - Hope - this person is still interested, excitement returns, they start to picture the move again, relief that they haven't lost the sale, the optimistic feeling comes back.

Offer 2 received - Disappointment - still a lower offer than expected but do they really want to go through the worry of losing the sale again, is it worth the risk to lose this buyer? The seller will seriously consider an offer at this stage as they won't like the feeling of potentially not selling. They may agree on the sale here or take the chance and reject it.

At this point, leaving time, (approximately 3/4 days), for the seller to think they have lost the sale will get them thinking that they will never sell. All their optimism and thoughts of moving are quickly disappearing. They are starting to feel a slight panic about not selling and starting to consider dropping the price.

Offer number 3 - The lifeline! Just as the seller has given up, a third and final offer is presented. This offer fills the seller with joy, excitement and hope. This time the offer seems reasonable it gives the seller the feeling that they have negotiated a great deal. They believe they have achieved far more than was initially offered, they are the winner, right? The feeling now is relief that another offer has come in and this time it seems like a decent offer, lower than what they wanted but much higher than what was initially offered.

When this offer is presented to the estate agent it's important to emphasise that it's the third and final offer and, if rejected, other properties will be focused upon. The agent will inform the seller and make it clear that this is their last chance to secure a sale.

Offer 3 accepted - In an ideal world the seller will now accept the offer. This doesn't always happen but, by following the steps above, there is a good chance of getting an offer accepted. If the offer is rejected it's advisable to inform the agent that the offer stands until another property is secured. Asking the agent to send over any similar properties they may have will emphasise that the negotiations are over, and the agent will typically advise the seller to accept the offer.

It's not uncommon for a seller to come back and accept an offer at a later date and it's worth checking in with the agent every couple of weeks to let them know an offer still stands.

Offer 1 - Is best in the form of an email.

Offer 2 - This offer can be verbal and should be approximately half of the amount between the amount initially offered and the asking price. When this offer is submitted, emphasising that numbers are having to be stretched and the deal is becoming very tight, makes an estate agent think that there won't be another offer. Remember an estate agent wants to sell properties. Again, this offer should not be a round number.

Offer 3 - The third and final offer, this should be the amount initially written down and when submitted it needs to be clearly stated that this is the final offer.

The valuation renegotiation

After an offer is accepted it's the job of the mortgage advisor to liaise with the lender to organise a valuation on the property. This is when the lender will officially agree to lend on the agreed purchase price, or not.

If the agreed purchase price is lower than the actual market value of the property the lender's valuer will value the property at the agreed purchase price, not the true market value.

If a valuation comes back lower than the agreed purchase price, then a renegotiation is advised. If a lender down values a property an investor will be required to pay the difference between the agreed purchase price and the loan amount on top of other associated costs.

At this stage, if a property is down valued it's advisable to contact the seller (vendor or estate agent) and to ask them to reduce the agreed purchase price to align with the lender's valuation. Explaining that the lender will only cover 25% (if a 75% loan to value mortgage product is being used) of the purchase price. The fact that the property price has been agreed above its value is often enough information to get the reduction needed.

Typically, agents and sellers will be somewhat understanding if a property is down valued and are often willing to align the agreed purchase price. However, if a seller refuses to re-negotiate and adjust the price an investor will have a decision to make as to whether to proceed or not.

If the decision is made to proceed then the numbers should be re-calculated factoring in the increased personal amount required.

The RICS re-negotiation

Once the agreed purchase price aligns with the lender's valuation, it is advisable to have a survey and valuation completed on the property. We will look into surveys in chapter 17.

A RICS report could highlight serious issues making the property unattractive, or the report may simply highlight small, insignificant problems that were visible on viewing. This is another opportunity to renegotiate, whether the issues highlighted are insignificant or not.

A detailed survey will highlight issues that may not have been identified when viewing the property. These points can be used to re-negotiate the purchase price down further.

Another attempt to re-negotiate will typically trigger the anger emotion with the seller and treading cautiously is advised. The seller typically won't want to lose the sale however if pushed too far, they may withdraw and put the property back on the market.

If there are issues raised that were not visible on viewing nor that formed part of the initial negotiation email and that will cost, it's advisable to go back and renegotiate.

The request for a further reduction is best done via email by highlighting direct quotes from the survey which will prove the points raised and add weight to the request. Again, offering slightly lower than the reduction amount desired will leave room to negotiate and meet in the middle.

Although this step often feels like a step too far, "if you don`t ask you don't get", it's always worth a shot but remember: push too far and you may lose the property.

It's worth noting that the seller will typically ask for a copy of the survey so it's wise to be truthful and accurate with presenting issues and highlighting problems.

SIXTEEN

Offer accepted

O nce an offer is accepted, the first step is to notify all key stakeholders. It's good practice and most efficient to send a group email to the following:

- Mortgage advisor.
- Solicitor.
- Estate Agent.

It's possible to save time and to eliminate numerous emails being sent back and forth by including a contact and company name, office address, phone number and email address of all parties involved so everyone has direct contacts and details for each other.

The email is to notify all parties that an offer has been accepted. The property address, agreed purchase price and contact details should also be included.

The estate agent should send out a memorandum of sale to you and both solicitors involved. However, they won't notify your mortgage broker and by you getting there first, it shows your professionalism and commitment to buying, this will come in useful later if you renegotiate.

> **Top Tip** - Speak separately to your solicitor; ask them to open a file but to hold off on the searches until further notice. The solicitor will send out initial paperwork, a list of their costs and request payment to start the searches. Simply tell them you will pay and complete the paperwork once you are happy with the results of a survey.
>
> Although with this technique there is a risk of annoying the seller and estate agent and of course losing the property, no costs will have been incurred. You are then able to check the surveys to ensure the property and price are still desirable.
>
> The survey may highlight issues with the property that make it no longer attractive and by holding back the solicitor, an investor will avoid losing money.
>
> Please note this is a risky technique, as estate agents may realise soon enough that there has been no commitment; however, if pulled off, the technique creates a very strong position to re-negotiate once surveys are obtained. If a vendor won't re-negotiate when the time comes, it's possible to walk away without incurring too much cost.

Behind the scenes, the mortgage adviser will start working on getting the loan processed and now they have the agent's contact details they will be able to organise access to the property for a mortgage valuation.

Once the agreed purchase price matches the lender's valuation it's time to have the property surveyed.

On receiving the survey results a decision to re-negotiate or move forward with the agreed purchase price will need to be made.

When happy with the purchase price, valuation and survey; the solicitor can be actioned to conduct searches.

The process is now in the solicitor's hands. They will liaise with the vendor's solicitors and conduct their investigations. It's advisable to check in with the solicitor bi-weekly to ensure everything is on track.

It typically takes six to eight weeks from an offer being accepted to the keys being released. Solicitors don't tend to communicate unless it's really necessary and it's typical for things to go quiet at this stage.

Whilst the case is with the solicitor it's often possible to gain access to the property (given there is a good relationship with the estate agents) to price up any work or to take photos to prepare a Rightmove advert.

> *Top Tip* – Write your own Rightmove advert. Preparing this information to pass to the chosen letting agent can speed things up dramatically and get a property advertised and let more quickly. Simply re-word the property description from the 'sales' advert to a 'let' advert.

Once searches and investigations are complete and the solicitor is happy to proceed with the sale, they will have contracts and paperwork that will need signing.

A solicitor will typically ask to meet face to face (this is usually compulsory if buying in a limited company) or they may post the documentation. It's important to read all of the information thoroughly and ask for clarity on anything that doesn't make sense.

The detail can be daunting to a newbie, however, it's the solicitor's job to translate any parts that aren't clear.

Once the paperwork is signed, a completion and exchange date will be set.

Next, the solicitor will usually ask for the deposit and stamp duty funds to be transferred to their account. The solicitor fees are usually billed separately and are requested after completion.

On completion day it`s normal to be contacted by the lender and solicitor to check if completion is agreed. The solicitor will then confirm when the transaction has taken place.

The keys will now be released from the Estate Agent.

Congratulations you have just bought an investment property.

SEVENTEEN

Solicitor

F inding the right solicitor is important and your choice will affect the process. Solicitors are known for being slow and unresponsive so it`s worth doing some research and due diligence before instructing anyone. It`s important to select a solicitor's firm who has a decent sized panel and who has experience in investment property purchases.

I interviewed Benn Hagger of Kew Law to get a better under-standing of what a new investor should look for in a solicitor. This is what Benn had to say:

What does a solicitor do?
They organise and prepare the documentation for the investor and then also check through the paperwork provided by the seller. Contracts are drawn up, title documents created, tenancy details are checked, searches are ordered, checked and requirements from the lender are processed. Basically, we do the 'behind the scenes' detective work to ensure a purchase is safe for the client and lender.

Is it beneficial for an investor to work with a property specialist solicitor?

All solicitors undergo at least seven years training and whichever solicitor you use you`ll have protection; however, it`s the experience and in-depth knowledge that you are looking for as a 'buy to let' investor. A specialist solicitor can make a real difference when it comes to investment properties.

As an example, an inexperienced investment solicitor may not possess the in-depth knowledge needed when properties are purchased with tenants in situ. Contracts need to be checked and documents served, to ensure the purchaser is fully covered in case anything goes wrong and if the tenant needs evicting in the future.

What should an investor look out for when selecting a solicitor?

The cost of being represented through the purchase of a property can vary and it`s important to be clear on what the overall cost and break down will be, before instructing a solicitor. A buy to let specialist solicitor with experience will be able to offer a more in-depth and tailored service to an investor. It is essential to have a good working business relationship with your solicitor to ensure they are able to translate often complicated legal jargon into laymen's terms for the investor to fully understand. The number of partners at the solicitor's firm is also important, we`ll touch on this later in the interview.

What are the common mistakes investors make before speaking to a solicitor?

By the time an investor is ready to instruct a solicitor, they feel that they are at the final stages of the purchase. Checking the legal paperwork is such an important part of the process and one that must be done correctly to ensure the deal stacks up for the investor. For example, investors often miss clauses in leases that stop their overall plan with the property; some properties have development restrictions and it`s easy for an investor to *have big plans but they are thwarted because paperwork checks were less than thorough.*

What costs are involved and how much should we be paying for a specialist property solicitor?

Costs vary from property to property and the area in which the solicitor is located will be a factor. There will be a cost difference if a property is occupied or if it's a leasehold property, this is due to the extra investigation and work to check the contracts.

As a general guide I would say you should expect to pay approx. £795 - £1200.

Is it better to buy a vacant property or one with a tenant in situ?

There is far more risk with tenanted properties, personally I would start with a vacant property. Selecting and referencing tenants isn't easy and not all agents are the best at it, so I would always rather trust my own agent to fill the property. At least when an investor's agent finds the tenant, they are responsible, and an investor should have a say and know what the selection criteria is. You also don't know if the previous landlord has breached any of the tenancy terms or if they have complied with the regulations. These factors can cause an investor a real problem down the line.

How does a solicitor help to keep an investor safe?

It's often easier for an investor to make mistakes when purchasing a property in cash as there is no lender criteria. It's the job of a solicitor to highlight all the risks to the investor whether buying with a mortgage or in cash. A solicitor is there to check all of the legal paperwork associated with the property and they are obligated to highlight all issues to an investor before an investor commits.

Does a chosen solicitor need to be on a lender's panel?

Yes, it's important to check if your solicitor is on the panel of the chosen lender. Most larger law firms work with the majority of common lenders. Some of the smaller law firms, with just one or a couple of partners, have limited access. It`s important to check as soon as possible as an investor can get a few weeks into the process and even have paid for searches when they then discover that the solicitor is not on the panel for the chosen lender.

What are my options if my solicitor doesn't work with the chosen lender?
A solicitor can apply to be on the panel; this is the easiest way. Or if an investor prefers, they can request a list of solicitors who work with the lender and proceed with another firm. This isn't ideal if costs have already been incurred as an investor will have to pay again. Having a solicitor apply to be on a panel will take time so it's important to check as early as possible.

Does the number of partners a firm has matter?
Yes, the more partners the better. Partners at law firms tend to specialise in different areas and having specialists in all areas helps to provide an in-depth service. Basically, the more heads around the table the better. Also, if a firm has a few partners they tend to be on more panels.

How long does the buying process take?
It varies. It depends on how quickly the buyer and seller submit their paperwork, how quickly the local council is at returning searches and of course how pro-active the solicitor is. I would say anywhere from six weeks to twelve weeks. If everything was returned on time and the process went smoothly it can all be completed in six weeks. Leasehold properties add time as leases need to be checked and there is a management company to also deal with.

Do I need to meet with my solicitor face to face?
It`s not always essential however things need to be done correctly due to the risk of fraud. Some solicitors insist they must meet a client face to face, or they may ask to see some original

documents. We like to meet our clients and if they are local, they often pop in to meet us. Meeting face to face really helps with long term relationship building and a quick 30-minute meeting can make a real difference and save a great deal of time with purchasing properties.

Documents can be posted, and signatures can be witnessed at post offices or other law firms so it's not essential but recommended.

My solicitor charges for phone calls and emails is this right?

You do need to be careful who you instruct. At Kew Law we work on a fixed fee so unless anything untoward crops up then an investor knows the full fee before we start work. Some firms do see communication via phone, letter or email as extra work and charge but this should always be part of the service. A quick call or email to ask a question or a chat every two weeks for an update should always be included but it sometimes isn't.

What's the best advice you could give for investors looking for a solicitor?

Have a chat with the solicitor first. Explain what you are trying to achieve, how you like to communicate, where you need the most help and get a feel to ascertain whether your communication styles and personalities match. It`s important to be open and honest from the outset to ensure you are both on the same page. I guess almost interview them before instructing, it's important to find a solicitor you can work with and trust, the buying process isn't quick and you`ll be working closely with this person. Every investor is different whether it's their 1st or 15th property; everyone has their own idea of what they want and how they work best and it's important to find the best solicitor to suit you.

Spending some time finding a top-notch solicitor will save time and reduce stress levels when an offer has been accepted.

> **Task:** Before you start offering on properties you should contact a property specialist solicitor. At this stage, it's about finding the right solicitor for you and simply informing them that you will soon be offering on some properties. All you need from your chosen solicitor is a verbal agreement that they are happy to legally represent you. Spend some time now finding a property specialist solicitor.

You can watch the full interview with Benn on the new2property You Tube channel by searching "why use a property specialist solicitor" and to find out more about Benn and to contact him visit the team page of the 'new2property' website. ***https://www.new2property.co.uk/team***

EIGHTEEN

Surveys

As a new investor, it can be very confusing researching and trying to find sound advice when it comes to surveys.

Below, I'll go through the different surveys available and provide some information on which surveys are best suited to the different property types.

The idea of a survey is to mitigate as much risk as possible and to eliminate the possibility of any nasty surprises or additional costs appearing once the sale completes.

I suggest having a survey completed on every property. I often hear people saying, do I need to get a survey? It's going to cost me X amount of money, I think it's okay, I've had a bit of a look around etc. I mostly reply with this question, "if you were going to buy a car that costs £30,000 and the dealer said you can have it fully checked over for £350. Before you hand over your money you will be given a list of everything that is wrong with the car and then you can renegotiate on the price, would you do it"? Of course you would, so why would an investment property be any different?

In my opinion, it will always be worth spending that small amount of money for peace of mind and the security of a surveyor's stamp vs the large amount of money that is to be invested.

There are a few surveys to choose from. Below I`ll break them down and go through them step by step to present a clear and concise indication of what each cover and which properties they are best suited to.

The surveys that I'm going to cover are:
- The mortgage valuation.
- The RICS condition report.
- The RICS Homebuyer's report with and without valuation.
- The home condition report.
- The building survey.

First, let's start with what a surveyor actually does.

A surveyor works from a list, they have a set criteria of information required which is dictated by the chosen survey or report.

The surveyor visits the property with their list, they check and report on everything in question to complete the survey. They then present the findings to whoever instructed them.

RICS stands for Registered Institute of Chartered Surveyors. This is a governing body that ensures that rules and regulations are followed by the surveyor carrying out the survey. Having a governing body ensures standardized best practice across the country and provides consistency in the reporting.

Mortgage valuation

If you own a residential property and used a mortgage to purchase it you will have some experience with mortgage valuations.

For any property that is purchased using a mortgage, the lender is required to check the value of the property matches the agreed purchase price. This valuation is safety and security for the lender.

A mortgage advisor will arrange the valuation with the lender on an investor's behalf. The investor has very little involvement at this stage other than receiving the valuation report when it's been completed.

If the property is valued equal to the agreed purchase price the lender will loan the full amount requested. However, if the report down values the property, an investor will need to decide whether to renegotiate on the agreed purchase price or to pay more of their own money.

It's important to note at this stage the lender won't issue a full list of faults or possible issues. The lender's valuation is not a full survey and all the lender is interested in is their own safety and security. The value of a property is calculated by averaging sold prices of a number of similar properties in the area. The condition of the property is taken into consideration, however the valuer does not go looking for issues or problems other than major factors that would affect the overall property value.

A basic valuation report is produced which will be forwarded to the mortgage advisor. The mortgage adviser will then, in turn, send the report on to the investor. The document will show the estimated property value and a reinstatement value: this is the cost of completely rebuilding the property if it was knocked down or burnt to the ground. This information will be requested when insuring the property.

The valuation is a good starting point, however it does not give the investor any real detail into the property's condition or highlight any potential problems.

Once the valuation report has been received and an investor is happy with the funds that are available, a decision will need to be made on whether to have a survey and, if so, which type.

Unlike the lender's valuation, an investor is responsible for organising a survey. It`s as simple as contacting a surveyor, paying for the report and providing the estate agent's contact details for them to gain access.

The RICS condition report
The most basic survey on offer is a RICS condition report.

This survey looks for current issues and problems that might occur in the future. When the report is produced it`s presented in a traffic light format:
- Green - no issue or problems
- Amber - highlights issues that are not serious or that will need attention over time rather than immediately.
- Red - require immediate attention.

This survey does not come with a valuation and is a very basic report. It does list defects and potential problems, however there is no advice provided on the fixes and the descriptions of the issues raised are basic.

This report is best suited for newer properties that are in good condition.

RICS homebuyers report
This report is a favourite of mine and it's also the most common amongst investors who are acquiring 'buy to let' properties.

This report is more detailed than the condition report and an investor will be issued a comprehensive list highlighting any current and potential issues within the property.

The report covers rot, damp, structural issues, subsidence, windows and doors, leaks, cracks, walls and ceilings and much more. The report provides information about the issues highlighted and give suggestions on how to rectify them.

It's worth noting that this report is non-intrusive, meaning furniture won't be moved, walls won't be drilled into, lofts won't be fully inspected, and carpets won't be lifted.

This report isn't the most in-depth, but it gives a really good, clear indication of what the property looks like past a simple viewing, as well as the potential issues and problems that will be present once the property is purchased.

This report can have an added bolt-on of a valuation, which I would always recommend. The valuation could be included, or it may be an additional extra. The valuation is completed at the same time as the survey and the issues raised will be taken into consideration when the valuation is calculated.

Armed with a survey and valuation report an investor has information that can be used to re-negotiate. There will typically be issues raised that would not have been visible on viewing and these issues can be used as bargaining power. The issues would, of course, come at a cost to the buyer once the property is purchased so it's important to carefully consider all highlighted issues.

The RICS homebuyers report is great for conventional properties that are in 'okay' condition.

If a property needs a substantial renovation or a lot of work this might not be the best survey.

Home Condition Survey

The Home Condition Survey is one step up from the homebuyer's report and is slightly different as it's conducted by the Residential Property Survey Association, not RICS.

This survey provides a full in-depth, detailed report into the issues and problems within a property.

The report is colour coded and photos as well as diagrams of the issues are presented. There is further detail provided with this report such as the area's broadband speed and information on the property's boundaries.

There isn't a valuation option with this report and it's mainly good for properties that are of standard construction, in relatively good condition.

Again, this report is non-intrusive, but it is a very comprehensive report, one that will provide detail to consider and analyse before moving forward with a purchase.

RICS building survey

This survey takes into consideration the structure of the property. It provides in-depth, granular detail on all specific issues and gives a full explanation and a time scale of how long it would take to rectify the concerns raised. It also outlines what the result would be if a highlighted issue isn't fixed.

The report highlights issues on a scale 1-3 and this survey is intrusive, walls are drilled into, floorboards lifted, lofts fully examined, under carpets and behind furniture etc.

This is the most in-depth survey available.

A building survey does not come with a valuation, but it will provide absolute peace of mind for an investor.

This survey is suited best to older properties, or properties requiring a full renovation.

I would advise that an investor has a survey completed on all investment property simply to mitigate risk and for peace of mind.

Surveys are priced in line with the size of the property, the location and survey type. Different companies charge different amounts, and this can vary a great deal so I suggest shopping around.

It's important to do a due diligence check on the surveyors; some call clients once the survey is completed and some are quicker than others to report back. Although the report is standardised the service isn't; so shop around and choose wisely.

NINETEEN

Insurance

Insurers will typically require the information listed below, to provide an insurance quote on a 'buy to let' property.

- Has the property been purchased in a company or personal name?
- When is the property due to exchange?
- When will the property be occupied?
- What is the rebuild value of the property?
- If insuring whilst the property is empty a brief description of any work and associated costs.
- Is the property of standard construction?
- Are there any flat roofs?
- Has the property ever suffered from cracking, subsidence or movement?

Top Tip: When insuring an investment property you will be asked for the rebuild cost. The rebuild cost is the amount it would cost to completely rebuild your home if it was destroyed beyond repair. It includes the price of labour and materials. You can check the rebuild costs of up to 5 properties for free on the BIC website:

> *https://calculator.bcis.co.uk/*
> The external floor area measurement is needed to run the report, which can be found on an EPC certificate. If you don`t have access to an EPC certificate you can view it on the Government ministry of housing website:
> *https://www.epcregister.com/*

I interviewed Josh Munt of Insurance Desk. In the interview, I ask Josh all the questions an investor needs to know before taking out investment property insurance. This is what Josh said:

What does an insurance broker do?
An insurance broker is there to match clients with insurers. By using a broker you should expect to get an additional service and value. As brokers are not insurers themselves, they can offer advice on policies and assist if any claims are made. It's a broker's job to ensure the insured is fully covered, that they understand the policy and that the product best suits their needs. It`s common for policy holders to have not read their product wording and to have little understanding of what their cover is: this is where a broker comes in. A broker should explain endorsement conditions, warranties and any clauses in the wording.

Can an insurance broker offer products from all insurers?
A broker will have access to multiple insurers and can compare products on a client's behalf, they usually have a panel of insurers that they work with and the more established brokers will have a good number of insurers to choose from.

Why would you use an insurance broker?
Unless you are an expert in insurance you won't know the best product to suit your needs, investors rely on a solicitor to cover the legalities, a mortgage broker to find the best mortgage product, a letting agent to find the best tenants so why would insurance be any different? A great broker will not only find the

most competitive product but also one that covers everything an investor wants.

It's easy to fall foul when selecting insurance policies and product wording can be confusing. It's the job of a broker to explain the terms and to ensure the investor is fully protected with complete piece of mind.

How much will an insurance broker cost me?

An insurance broker will charge an admin fee and that is made clear in the policy. Investors often don't realise that the majority of online companies: 'Go Compare' for example' are brokers; they charge an admin fee as well. However, with an online company, you don't actually receive the benefit or value of working with a broker.

What should I look for in a broker?

A decent broker should explain their costs and go through any policies in depth before taking payment. Claims is an important area: although we all hope never to need our insurance, if anything does happen, a good broker will be there to support. They will liaise with the insurer and a loss assessor and help manage the claim. They will ensure that you receive everything that you are entitled to. It's a broker's job to question and challenge information if it doesn't seem right.

The cost of a broker is also important: although the policy needs to be right, no one wants to pay more than they need to.

What is the most common mistake by investors regarding insurance policies?

One of the biggest is rebuild values: investors will set their rebuild value the same or less than the purchase price and don't realise that this amount covers many areas. The rebuild will include clearing all debris from the site, architects, planning agents, professional fees and much more, the rebuild cost will be stated on a lender's valuation or you can check it out on the BICS website but it's almost always higher than the purchase price and most investors get this wrong.

Occupancy is another area where investors slip up, if a property is vacant between tenancies then it's important to report it to the broker. Most policies allow 30 days after the stated time frame when the insurance cover changes to a minimum cover. A broker can keep the insurer up to date with the occupancy and negotiate the cover whist a property is empty. It`s possible to get cover that allows 90 days and if this is important then a broker can add this to the list of criteria.

The employment status of tenants is also often stated on policies so if a change of tenants happens and the tenants go from employed to unemployed the policy terms could be breached.

What's the most common claim that you deal with?

Escape of water, it`s a nightmare and causes insurers a real headache. The problem is that you can't really stop it happening and when it does, it causes huge damage. The majority of the time it comes from burst pipes and when that happens it often involves removing tiles, kitchen units, flooring etc. Whilst it's being sorted, tenants have to move out, and what was a small leak often turns in to a very expensive claim. This issue commonly happens during winter when a property is being renovated or when empty between tenancies. As previously mentioned, if a property is empty then most policies drop to minimum cover which doesn't include water damage or burst pipes!

What should an investor do if they have a claim?

The first step is to fix the immediate issue and to try and prevent further damage. Then call the insurance broker, a broker will then be able to assist and advise on the next steps. You could opt to work with a loss assessor who can manage the end to end process for you; but a broker will explain all of this when the time comes.

Any final words

The property market is changing day by day and there are many new and interesting strategies cropping up so make sure you let your insurance company or broker know exactly how you are operating: is the property an HMO, a serviced accommodation, a rent to rent etc.? If the policy isn't set up correctly and terms are breached, an insurance company won't pay out.

You can view the full interview with Josh on the new2property You Tube channel by searching for "Buy to let insurance explained"

TWENTY

Choose your letting agent

Finding the perfect letting agent to work with is up there on the "most important" list when it comes to setting up a property business. The decision on this matter can be the difference between a hassle-free hands-off investment and a huge hands-on headache.

It's worth spending some time finding an agent that not only excels in their field but also who compliments your working and management style.

> *Task:* Write down what skills and qualities you would ideally want in a business partner. Below you will find some suggestions to get you thinking.

- **Passion**: Ideally, the agent you decide to partner with should be just as passionate about their business as you are about yours.
- **Reliable**: You want a reliable agent to work with you and your tenants.

- **Compatibility**: Being compatible with your chosen agent will mitigate problems or conflict.
- **Strong relationship builder:** Property is a people business and any agent needs to be great with people.
- **Great communicator**: How do you like to best communicate, are you an emailer, a WhatsApp fan, or do you prefer to take calls?

Task: It's now time to contact the local letting agents in your area. Follow the steps below to help you find the perfect agent.

Initially, an efficient way to contact all local letting agents is to send a group email.

Googling 'letting agents' in an area will produce a list; some will have direct email addresses and others a contact form.

Although it takes some time to extract all the individual email addresses, it's a worthwhile task to ensure the perfect agent is found.

A great place to collate the email address is on the 'new2property' Deal Calculator spreadsheet where there is a tab already created with prompts for suggested information.

Branch Name	Office Email address	Contact Name	Contact Email Address	Contact Phone Number
Newton Fallowell	info@lettingagent.com	John Smith	john@letting.com	07 79 86 76 54

Once all contact details have been collated it's time to say "Hi". At this stage, using a blanket email using the Bcc function will suffice.

Although this might seem very impersonal the first contact is simply to test how responsive and reactive the different agents are.

Here is an example template that could be used to send out to all agents

Good afternoon,

I am hoping you can help me, I'm a property investor and will require the services of a reputable letting agent in the coming months.

I currently have an offer accepted on a 3-bed terrace house on xxx street, in xxx. The property is in great condition, has a modern bathroom and kitchen, uPVC windows and doors, a small enclosed garden and on-street parking.

Over the next 12 months, I plan to increase my portfolio size by an additional 5 properties and I'm looking for a letting agent to take on the full management of my portfolio.

I'm interested in your professional opinion on the possible rent that I could achieve from my property on xxx street. Please find attached the sales brochure for reference.

Would you also be able to provide me with information on your fully managed service including your commission/costs?

Can you also let me know if you are part of ARLA (Association of Residential Letting Agents), if you are members of the CMP (Client Money Protection) and if you are part of any redress schemes?

Thank you very much for your time; I look forward to hearing from you

Kind Regards

Once the template email is perfected it can also be dropped into any contact forms.

When an agent replies it's worth checking their reviews on the All Agents website to see what others have to say. *https://www.allagents.co.uk/*

If an agent doesn't reply it's a good indication of their service, some will call which is a good sign and shows they are keen to present their services.

When an agent does reply it's advisable to make notes on all interactions. The aim is to find the agent that fits the perfect business partner description written down earlier.

Here are some great follow up questions once conversations start:
- Can I have a full list of all your charges?
- Do you charge a percentage on maintenance jobs?
- How often do you routinely inspect properties?
- How many properties do you manage?
- Do you advertise on all the main portals including Rightmove and Zoopla?
- On receipt of rent, when do you pay the landlord?
- Which deposit protection scheme do you use?
- Do you have systems in place to track rental payments, repairs, compliance obligations etc?
- What is your staff to property ratio?
- Which Ombudsman Scheme are you a member of?
- Do you assign team members to landlords/portfolios?
- Do you undertake a check-in and check-out inventory, and mid-term property inspections?
- Is your key staff (Branch Manager as a minimum) NFOPP qualified?
- Do you have a website, fixed premises and a landline number?

- Are you VAT registered?
- Are you on the Data Protection Register?
- How will you market my property/find tenants?
- Do you have a team of tradespeople?
- How many staff and branch offices do you have?
- Are your principles (Director or Branch Manager) property investors/landlords themselves?
- How many years have you been operating?
- What are your procedures for evictions?
- What are your procedures for dealing with maintenance issues?

It's also acceptable to ask to speak to landlords who the agent currently works with. They will, of course, choose their trusted investors; however, if the agent cannot provide any it would cause concern.

Although you don't want to put agents off working with you by going over the top with your due diligence it's very important that you find an agent that you can fully trust to manage your portfolio.

TWENTY ONE

Pro Photos

Paying for a professional property photographer once an investment property is looking its best, will allow an investor to re-advertise instantly when a tenant gives notice. This will also eliminate the need to take photos with a tenant in situ later down the line.

It's advisable to budget approximately £100 per property depending on the location and the photographer used.

On the next page you can see some photos I have taken myself next to the same room photographed by a professional. Note the difference when they are professionally shot.

Conclusion

I`m sure, from reading this book, you can see that I am truly passionate about property, and that's because when you get it right, and you grow your portfolio, it can make a huge difference to your life. However, you look at it, money is a large part of life and there is no better vehicle for creating wealth than property.

The life you want to create can be fuelled by the property portfolio you build. And too often the actual reason people start investing - money, financial freedom, a better life for their kids, to leave a legacy - becomes just a dream.

That's because they don`t take action or they take the wrong action that will end in shattering their dreams.

All chapters in this book are designed to help you buy a safe, solid, sound and secure 'Buy To Let' investment property, and the journey of purchasing your first investment property will equip you to up-scale and grow in the future.

Having a profit generating property portfolio is the ultimate vehicle for creating the life you have always dreamed of. Society, the media, friends and family and all those who have knocked your confidence over time have conditioned you to believe that the rat race is the only way; your dreams have been eroded and doubt has set in. Negative influencers who have long given up on their dreams frequently offer advice to fill you with doubt which makes you second guess yourself and question if it's actually possible. You want your children to be happy, you want to provide for them and your family; you dream of a great, carefree relationship with your spouse with the money and time to enjoy life; but society trains us all to believe this is not possible without following the crowd. I`m here to tell you it is possible, those who don`t have the courage to go out and make their dreams a reality will continue to spread negativity and doubt and be no better off for it.

You can create long term wealth in property and my personal journey proves this.

Not only is building a profit generating property portfolio a great creator of wealth, it also develops skills in every other area of your life.

Running a business takes grit, drive and determination. The stakes are high, and the pressure is real. You will need to have stamina, be highly focused and get up every time you fall.

These traits will be tested and pushed to the limits, however, as you grow and build and get stronger these same traits will serve you in all areas of your life: from your physical and mental health, fitness and relationships.

The pressure will grow but so will you. Pressure is a fact of life and those who learn to perform under it become high achievers.

Failure doesn't occur to high achievers: they become more focussed and pressure simply ignites their resolve.

If you are serious about investing in property, then now is the time to take action. The best time to buy property is always NOW.

One last thing...

This is not "goodbye", but rather, "see you soon".

It's been an absolute pleasure being your mentor throughout this journey. I want to personally thank you for not only buying into 'new2property' as a brand but also to me as your 'Buy To Let' property mentor.

I really hope that this book has helped you achieve success and provided you with the tools and knowledge to continue as a confident and competent property investor.

I would love to hear about your success stories. Please send me your achievements and results. There is nothing better for me than hearing about your success.

Below you will find ways to keep in touch and up to date with what's happening in the property world, so subscribe, like, and don't be a stranger.

Follow us on You Tube "new2property" to get further insights and information on all things 'buy to let'.

Give us a like on Facebook "new2property" to get handy hints and tips dropped onto your news feed on a regular basis.

Follow us on Instagram @new2property to see what we are up to on a daily basis.

Congratulations...

You are now a knowledgeable and experienced property investor.

Thank you and the best of luck for your future in property.

Dan Coachafer

More resources for you

At 'new2property' we help new and experienced professionals invest in 'buy to let' property.

Clients develop practical knowledge and skills of how to build a profitable property portfolio that will create a positive lifestyle for them and their family.

We provide a one on one, six-month coaching and mentoring program *https://www.new2property.co.uk/program*

And an online: 'How to - Buy To course Let' course *https://new2property.thinkific.com/* for new and experienced investors.

Printed in Great Britain
by Amazon

54624713R00084